Health-Care
Entrepreneurship

Health-Care

Entrepreneurship

Embracing the Mindset and Skills for Competitive and Sustainable Healthcare Entrepreneurship

Chris Ehiobuche Ph.D.

To order additional copies of this book, contact:
Xlibris
844-714-8691
www.Xlibris.com
Orders@Xlibris.com
836995

To my parents and parents-in-law and in particular
Maria Jesus Sanchez Mendoza.

CONTENTS

Acknowledgments...ix
Preface...xi

Chapter 1   Overview of the American Health-Care System.................1
Chapter 2   Characteristics of the U.S. Health-Care System 11
Chapter 3   Challenges and Opportunities for Health-Care
             Entrepreneurs 19
Chapter 4   Starting a Health-Care Business 31

             Types of Health-Care Services...31
             Types of Business Entities...35
             How to Start a Health-Care Business...................................47

Chapter 5   Operational Logistic and Health-Care Supply
             Chain Management...61

             Health-Care Supply Chain Management Process 61

Chapter 6   Health-Care Technology and Innovations.........................73
Chapter 7   Medical Informatics, Data Science, Decision-
             Making, and Quality Improvement.............................83
Chapter 8   Practice Management 90

             Finance..91
             Compliance 91
             Information Technology..91
             Marketing 92
             Operations...92
             Models for Urgent Care 93
             Models for Outpatient..94
             Building and Retaining Patients' Panel...............................94

Chapter 9   Human Factors 97
Chapter 10   Insurance Companies and Other Regulatory Agencies...113
Chapter 11   Cash Flow, Revenue Management, and Return on
                 Investment 123

                 Cash Flow 123
                 Revenue Cycle Management..126
                 Return on Investment (ROI) 128

Chapter 12   Growth Strategy 130
Chapter 13   Burnouts 140
Chapter 14   Mindset—Becoming an Entrepreneur: From Faith
                 to Action 149

References 159

ACKNOWLEDGMENTS

Thank you to

- all the team of researchers who supported this project,
- all the reviewers for their time and contributions,
- all the staff of Faith Family Health Care for all their help,
- all my colleagues at Berkeley College,
- all my colleagues at Metropolitan College of New York, and
- all my colleagues and MHAL program students at Stockton University.

Preface

Medical care is one of the most important needs of human beings; without good health, any other achievement is useless. Health care is about providing medical services, products, and equipment to extend, protect, and enhance the quality of human life. This is why there are a number of lucrative business opportunities in the health-care industry in medical and nonmedical services. It is indeed a billion-dollar industry that is still growing since the need for strong health-care services has been increasing over time. On top of that, COVID-19 has signaled the need for further improvement in this sector as it has posed certain challenges.

Health care is one of the most strictly regulated sectors since it is directly related to precious human lives. Since you are interested in becoming a health-care entrepreneur, you must ensure that you obtain an obligatory license before you launch your health-care business. In some cases, you may need to get certain certification to obtain the license.

Identifying new business opportunities is challenging during the COVID-19 pandemic. However, technology has opened up many new opportunities in the health-care sector. In fact, digital transformation for patient care has become an important aspect of this pandemic.

Today health facilities are leaving behind manual procedures and are more inclined to implement technological devices that can help medical operations and reduce the margin of errors in other admirative tasks. Indeed, COVID-19 has caused great damage to world economies. However, the pandemic has also enhanced opportunities in the health-care sector.

COVID-19 has indeed caused substantial economic disruption, but long-term effects on business and innovation can be alleviated through taking steps to support present start-ups and the creation of new firms.

In fact, it is the best time for entrepreneurs to enter the industry. If you notice, you can identify that recession is the time when restructuring and innovation in businesses occur, leading to a more resilient and robust economy.

On the one hand, new business registrations drop during recessions; on the other hand, many innovative start-ups have emerged during periods of crisis, for example, Dropbox, Uber, Airbnb, WhatsApp, and Groupon, among others; these businesses were initiated during or right after the global financial crisis. Alibaba's Taobao started during the SARS outbreak in China in 2003. Crisis surely poses challenges, but it also provides new opportunities for entrepreneurs since they help address the issues and limitations caused by adverse conditions as they respond to the situation innovatively.

Business opportunities for entrepreneurs help them introduce essential innovations. In the health-care industry, opportunities and innovations can translate into telehealth, data mining, medical equipment, medical tourism, and remote personal care, among others. Certainly, these are not easy times, but there is a great potential that you have to identify and avail of. In fact, the purpose of writing this book is to help you see a wide range of business opportunities in this sector.

CHAPTER 1

Overview of the American Health-Care System

America's health care system provides some of the finest doctors and more access to vital medications than any country in the world. And yet, our system has been faltering for many years with the increased cost of health care.

—Paul Gillmor

Health care is one of the essential needs of human beings in every country, and its provision is one of the core responsibilities of the government. The developing countries may not have robust health-care systems, which is obvious. Also, it is believed that developed countries have reliable and effective health-care systems, and they must have; however, a few flaws can still exist in the health-care systems of the developed countries, and the United States is no exception in this regard. I don't mean to say that the U.S. health-care system has failed to serve the nation, not a long shot; however, there is always room for improvement, and this is where health-care entrepreneurs can find their window of opportunity. As a health-care entrepreneur, you must see that health care is an everlasting sector and will grow further.

When you have set your mind to becoming a health-care entrepreneur, the first thing you need is to go through an overview of the current system. This activity will help you see how the system is working and if there are gaps in it that you can fill with your entrepreneurial business ideas and

1

strategies. Thus, I'll show you an overview of the U.S. health-care system in this chapter, covering history, components, scope and complexities, and the possible future—the future where you could be a major player in the system.

Our health-care system was shaped by the core values of the American people, which include individualism, fairness, equality, and liberty. Liberty prevails and will continue to be the ethical justification for health-care reforms in the system. Liberty signifies privacy, choice, civil rights, and individuality so that Americans can have freedom of choice in selecting their physicians and health-care plans. Thus, it was with these values in the governmental system where key legislative acts were born and that shaped the health-care system.

The History

An advocate and social activist, Dorothea Dix, was one of the first people to present the health-care proposal to the government in *1854*. [1] She wanted the government to build asylums for the indigent mental patients, the blind, and the deaf and a proviso of other health-care services for the poor. The bill was actually passed in both houses of the Congress, but it was ultimately vetoed by Pres. Franklin Pierce, who claimed that social welfare was a state's responsibility and not of the federal government.

Later in *1865*, at the end of the Civil War, the government established what became known as the Freedmen's Bureau, which built hospitals and employed doctors to treat the sick and dying and the former slaves in the South. [2] From *1865* to *1870*, the Freedmen's Bureau treated over one million former slaves. But unfortunately, by *1870*, hospitals in the South had to start closing due to rising riots and violence from a small group of rebels called the Ku Klux Klan. For the next seventy years, the topic of health care became a major talking point in the government.

In *1933*, after the Great Depression, millions of Americans couldn't afford medical care. Hence, Pres. Franklin D. Roosevelt attempted to create publicly funded health-care programs, [3] but he was vehemently opposed by groups like the American Medical Association (AMA), a powerful group of physicians. The AMA claimed that such programs would be considered compulsory. Because of vehement opposition, Roosevelt had to drop those programs from his New Deal.

Later in *1945*, Roosevelt's successor, Harry S. Truman, tried to pass the Universal Health-Care Bill, [4] but he, too, was opposed by the AMA, who is now using a term that, to this day, still strikes fear into the heart of many Americans, and that is *socialized medicine*. [5] By invoking socialism, the AMA started stirring up fears that America was going to leave behind its capitalist roots and start going the way of a communist regime. The excuse of socialized medicine was also the reason that Lyndon B. Johnson couldn't pass a universal health-care bill in the *1960s*. Despite the opposition from the AMA and some conservative republicans, Johnson managed to pass what became to be known as Medicare in *1965*. [6]

Throughout the *1970s*, there were multiple attempts to get the Universal Health-Care Bill passed. One of the leading advocates of universal health care was Sen. Ted Kennedy. He proposed the Health Security Act, which was a single-payer system that would provide coverage to almost every single American. Again, unfortunately, the bill never made it out of Congress. [7]

Jumping into the *1990s*, Bill and Hillary Clinton attempted a major health-care reform by introducing the American Health Security Act (AHSA) in *1993*. [8] The plan proposed health care for all Americans via private insurers in a regulated market. Furthermore, employers would be required to provide health care to their employees and pay 80 percent of the premiums, and health-care plans were required to provide a minimum level of benefits. However, in *1994*, after disputes between the supporters of the bill and its opponents who claimed that the AHSA gave more power to the insurers and took away the rights of the patients to choose their own doctor, the bill was killed.

A few years back, the Patient Protection and Affordable Care Act was signed into law by President Obama in *March 2010*. [9] Democrats praised the plan, saying that with the passing of the Affordable Care Act, more Americans would be able to get health-care insurance. Meanwhile, the Republicans opposed and claimed socialized medicine.

The American Association for Labor Legislation (AALL) was the first to propose an insurance program that would provide sick pay, medical and maternity coverage for women and wives of men, and a small death benefit. But there were many opposing this program, especially employers, who were the primary payers. To encourage employers to take part in an employer-based health insurance program, public policy choice such as the

Revenue Act of 1942 and the National War Labor Board ruling in 1943 stated that employee benefit plans would be tax deductible. [10]

The AMA played a major role in the maintenance of the employer-based health insurance system and vehemently imposed and prevented the passing of any bill that intended to implement national health insurance, such as the 1943 Wagner-Murray-Dingell Bill. [11] Disapproval stemmed from the group's fear that increased government control would eliminate their autonomy and power. With relentless opposition to and repeated failure of reform proposals, an employer-based health insurance system remained intact and continued to grow.

Regrettably, the system created a huge gap between the insured and the uninsured. Employer-based health care left millions of people uninsured for a variety of reasons, including unemployment and loss of jobs. Being self-employed, some employers did not offer a health coverage plan; and even if they wanted to, they could simply not afford to pay for it. Many companies minimized benefits because they either could not or did not want to cover premium expenses. National health insurance could have dissolved this issue, but Americans desired neither increased taxes nor increased government involvement. The employer-based health insurance system minimized the government's role and allowed citizens to retain individualism, but it did so at the expense of inadequate coverage and care.

The Components

The U.S. health-care system is similar to that of many other developed countries. It is a blend of public and private components. Almost all care is provided by the private sector. Though a few hospitals are administered by the government, most of them are run by private organizations. About 70 percent of hospitals are nonprofit. Hence, most of the physicians work for private organizations as well.

Other components are also in the private sector (i.e., pharmaceutical and medical device firms). Research work is sponsored by the public as well as private sources, whereas the private sector makes higher contributions. The U.S. expenditure on medical research accounts for the vast majority of R&D spending in the world. When compared with other countries, we can see that the difference lies in how the U.S. government provides citizens access to the system. We can say that the United States is anachronistic to some extent in this regard.

Until recently, almost 15 percent of the people in the United States were uninsured. It suggested that if they faced a medical need, they would have to bear the medical bills on their own. Everyone must know that our system is really expensive; it is somewhat problematic because it means that there is a large number of people who remain devoid of health-care services. They don't get the care they need, meaning that a great number of American citizens are being failed by the authorities.

About 60 percent of U.S. citizens get health insurance from their employers. These health insurance plans generally don't charge them various amounts based on factors like age, gender, or past medical history. However, they mostly cover preventive care, care if a person gets sick, and drug prescriptions. Plans can vary in terms of how much people have to pay out of pocket for them.

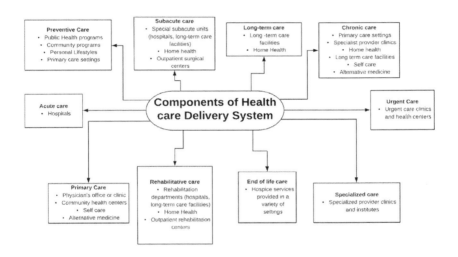

Figure 1.1

About 15 percent of American citizens are covered by Medicare, in which most are the elderly. Medicare is a national social insurance program that is managed by the federal government. It is the closest to what most people refer to as the single-payer system, where all people are covered by one type of insurance. However, this Medicare system seems a little complicated.

Medicare Part A covers a person if they are hospitalized. It is free for people over the age of sixty-five, so almost no one gets Medicare Part A.

Medicare Part B covers outpatient services. It is different for people who are still getting insurance from their jobs. It is a pretty low deductible and has coinsurance of 20 percent. It covers almost everything, including all tests and procedures, even outside the hospital, and also the required medical equipment.

Private companies offer additional Medigap policies to cover the copay and added benefits. Nearly all people purchase at least one of these two additional covers so that they will not need to pay a higher cost for their health care.

Medicare Part C, also called Medicare Advantage, is an option for a private firm to offer Medicare-like advantages that are even better than the government's plan. The recipients of Medicare can choose Medicare Advantage in place of the traditional Medicare because of more benefits; almost a quarter of people go for this option.

Medicare Part D offers plans that cover prescription drugs. They are managed by private insurers, but they are approved and paid for by the federal government. The cost of Medicare in 2013 was about $536 billion.

The other big government program is Medicaid. Unlike Medicare, Medicaid is a state-based program. It is actually supposed to provide health-care coverage for the poor people in society. Some minimal federal guidelines are set for Medicaid, and then each state gets to implement it as it sees fit. Some states are more generous than others. Normally, Medicaid covers the people who are at the low end of the socioeconomic spectrum.

Traditional Medicaid must cover kids under six years of age to 133 percent of the federal poverty line and kids six to eighteen years to 100 percent of the poverty line. The State Children's Health Insurance Plan (SCHIP) increases up to 300 percent of the poverty line in most states. Traditional Medicaid also covers pregnant women up to 133 percent of the poverty line and parents to the 1996 welfare levels. Moreover, it covers the elderly and the disabled who receive Supplemental Security Income (SSI).

There is a noteworthy point that adults without children are not mentioned in it, and they cannot obtain Medicaid in most states, including the poorest ones. Those 1996 welfare levels can be so low that if in Arkansas a couple with two children is making $3,820 a year, they are considered as too rich to get Medicaid. Though a few states seem to be generous, parents must be essentially poor in most states to get Medicaid.

The Medicaid expansion in the Affordable Care Act was supposed to fix this concern and offer the plan to people hitting 138 percent of the poverty line irrespective of having children or not. However, it has not happened yet. Because of the Supreme Court's decision that made the Medicaid expansion optional, many states refused it, leaving an additional five million people with low income with no insurance.

In 2009, Medicaid covered more than sixty million Americans. About one in three children and births are covered by Medicaid. In 2011, Medicaid cost was about $414 billion. [12]

There is also the Veterans Health Administration, which is a government-run system that provides care to veterans and TRICARE, the military health insurance program that applies to some veterans, military personnel and retirees, and dependents. TRICARE works more like private insurance.

Scope and Complexity

If we look at the list of countries that have the best health-care systems, we'll likely see Sweden, Denmark, Canada, Germany, Switzerland, Japan, the Netherlands, and Singapore somewhere on the list. But how are these lists compiled? They are compiled by taking into account the following factors regarding the overall health-care system:

- Total spending
- Quality of services
- Availability
- Effectiveness

Another important factor on this list is how much people have to pay for health-care services, a core reason we do not find the USA on this list of the best health-care systems. The American media often tells us that being sick in the United States can bankrupt a family, but how does this actually happen?

According to CNBC, medical bills can cause many problems in the USA. Their report stated that medical bills are the leading cause of bankruptcy in the United States, but the number is indefinable. [13] President Obama said in 2009 that the medical bills caused bankruptcy in the United States every thirty seconds. [14] These numbers have been contested, and skeptics tell us that there is always more to bankruptcy in these cases with just medical bills. Maybe those bills were just a straw that broke the camel's back. However, there is one thing we can take from the stats, even if not entirely accurate; it is that America, a country so developed and rich, might not be doing a good enough job looking after its citizens.

Recent research showed that the United States spent 17.9 percent of the GDP on the health-care system in 2016, which amounts up to $3.3 trillion. [15] This estimates an expenditure of almost $10,348 on every sick person.

We might have seen that Americans shop for health insurance like anything else. Another research observed that around 156 million Americans are insured provided by their employer, which is called private insurance. [16] There is also a publicly funded medical care for older people, the disabled, and the poor. Around 120 million Americans are part of these schemes, which is why this system has been called a public-private hybrid system.

The money involved in the health care of the United States is unbelievable. CNBC wrote in 2018 that only 39 percent of Americans have enough savings to cover a $1,000 emergency. [17] Experts tell us that Americans should downgrade their lifestyle in case they get sick even if they have insurance because going bankrupt could mean that they might not get a loan again or be able to rent a house or even get a job.

The reasons why most people in the United States are not able to pay their medical bills are most probably assumed to be

- administrative costs,
- drug costs,
- possible lawsuit,
- wages of health-care workers,
- new technologies, and
- diverse costs of the medical institutions.

The *Washington Post* once wrote an article stating that America has the most expensive but least effective health care in the developed world. [18] This is the reason why the country is not on any best health-care list. This is a huge debate in the United States of America, and we might have been quite critical about it.

The Future

A digital transformation is sweeping all industries, and health care is the second least digitized industry in the United States. According to a recent study, only the construction industry is less digitized than health care in the United States. [19] Electronic health records (EHRs) have digitized billing, and clinical encounters are already in use, but they only contain 80 percent of the required data, which is why there is a need to go beyond the EHR technology.

Digitalization of the patients' data and their health maintenance should be the next thing for consideration. We must collect, use, and analyze new sources of data such as the following:

- Social data
- Genomic data
- Encounter data
- Biometric data
- Outcomes data
- Microbiome data

AI and machine learning breakthroughs in new technology will enable new levels of care improvement. This could include diagnostic care, predictive care, and prescriptive care that are even faster, cheaper, and better. Data is the key to the future. If the public or government sector will not lead this, the private will, where employers will be the first to take the initiative.

New technology has the power to transform health-care systems. A survey conducted by the GE Healthcare Commission asked ten thousand people who were mostly patients around the world about how they want to see the technology to be used in the future to improve health care. The reply was noteworthy. People were mostly concerned about the cost of health care. Moreover, they wanted shorter waiting times, increased access to health care, and a better quality of health-care services.

So how can technology help in making the health care's future in the United States brighter? The foremost priority of the U.S. health-care sector should be to use technology to deliver quicker diagnostic results to patients. Participants of the GE health-care survey were of the idea that having an updated and safe technology could improve health care.

By allowing doctors instant access to patients' medical data and images, things can become easier for health-care workers. Having shorter queuing times in the emergency room can help the patients and attendants exert less energy and save time.

The GE health-care survey observed that 87 percent of people believed that using technology to monitor health on the go will be the most important medical innovation, followed by the recording of patient data in digital form and using analytical tools to reduce the number of cancellations and delays in operations. [20] Therefore, investments should be made in technology to help customers and patients transform health care.

CHAPTER 2

Characteristics of the U.S. Health-Care System

America's health care system is the most complicated and expensive in the world.

—Christy Turlington

In the previous chapter, we looked at the factors that affect the health-care system of a country, how American citizens manage to pay their health-care bills, and how some people are left out of the system. In this chapter, we will go through the major characteristics of the U.S. health-care system.

As a health-care entrepreneur, learning about the characteristics of your target field will also guide you to develop innovative ideas. There are many factors and ideologies that shape the U.S. health care, such as social and political environment, growth of economy and technology, and cultural values. Let me tell you one thing that you never, as a health-care entrepreneur, take any point lightly. Thus, you need to be detail oriented and read between the lines.

The primary objective of a health-care system is to provide all citizens with cost-effective and quick health-care services that meet specific preestablished standards of quality. Most developed countries have national health insurance programs, and these are referred to as universal access while they focus on the primary objective. The systems in other developed countries are run by the government to provide routine and primary health care to the citizens. However, the U.S. health-care system is different from the other systems in the world. It does not currently have a national health insurance program that provides universal access. All Americans are not entitled to routine and basic health-care services. However, they are entitled to a public defender.

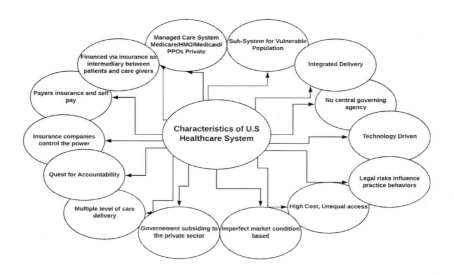

Figure 2.1

Let's see the main characteristics of our system that make it different. This way, you will be able to see the window of opportunity to develop your entrepreneurial ideas in this field.

1. No Centralization

There is no central governing agency in the U.S. health-care system like other developed countries. It could be run by a private agency as well, yet there isn't any. This is why there is less integration and coordination. A central system is less complex and less costly; however, the government or private sector does not seem to be on the same page in this regard.

Also, centrally controlled systems work better than a decentralized system. Since they have all the systems integrated well with each other, they are highly coordinated and productive. On the other hand, not being centralized adds a lot of complexity. First, payments have to transfer hands, which is usually done by insurance that deals with the delivery mechanism. Diverse organizations, programs, and systems within the government cause chaos, such as having Medicaid and Medicare at the same time.

Health care is financeable publicly and privately; therefore, this interaction between public and private financers adds up to the mess. Private insurance, through employers or individually purchased insurance, acts similarly to governmental programs. But of course, they are different, and many people avail both.

2. Obsession with Technology

The word *obsession* may offend some people, but it is a fact in our system. It focuses on curative and acute care, while preventive care itself is not given due care. The U.S. health-care system invests largely in research and innovations in new medical technology, which may help create fancy and high-tech equipment and services. This innovation could include robotic arms for surgery and new drugs. In fact, patients in the United States who are lucky enough to have access to health care demand all this fancy equipment.

Now there are shrinking resources not only for these new technology tools but also for all kinds of care. Technology has been implemented with some success, but it is obviously overused. The cost of this botched technology is not trivial but is mostly indirect. Its implementation affects employers and employees as they have to pay for it in their health plans. However, this is some good news for health-care entrepreneurs who are big on technology.

3. Expensive and Unequal

The U.S. system is high in cost and has unequal access for all U.S. citizens. Unfortunately, it is also average in the outcome compared with other developed countries. The United States spends more money than any other developed country on its health-care system, but much of it is consumed by research and technology as I mentioned earlier. Therefore, the costs are high at an alarming rate.

Being costly in its very nature, the U.S. health-care services are not accessible to every citizen, which causes great disparity. Therefore, less expensive health-care services are availed by most people. Financing and insurance are the key forecasters of access. Since many U.S. citizens have limited access to primary care, they are not even contributing any money to the system.

Access to care in the United States is limited to those who have health insurance under an employer or those who are covered under a government program like TRICARE, Medicaid, and so on or who can afford to pay on their own. This disparity needs to be dealt with by either the government or health-care entrepreneurs for being a fellow citizen. And who knows if your entrepreneurial idea can work for this purpose?

4. Imperfect Market Condition

The delivery of health care under imperfect market conditions is another hallmark of the U.S. health-care system, and this is how market justice comes into play. When there are national health-care plans, patients can have multiple options in choosing their health-care providers, but true economic market forces are nearly absent. In the United States, the delivery of services is mostly in private hands, but health care is partly administered by free market forces. Both the delivery and consumption of health care don't fairly meet the basic tests of a free market. Thus, we can describe the U.S. health-care system as an imperfect market.

In a free market, patients, who act as buyers, and providers, who act as sellers, act autonomously. Patients should have a choice among providers that may be based on price and quality of services. Hypothetically, prices are negotiated between health-care payers and providers, whereas the payer is mostly not the patient but Medicare, Medicaid, and so on. Since prices are set by agencies that are external to the market, they are not freely administered by the forces of supply and demand.

In a free market, there is unrestricted competition among health-care service providers, again based on price and quality. On the whole, free competition does exist among health-care providers, but the consolidation of purchase power in the hands of private health plans forces providers to promote integrated delivery systems (IDSs) in terms of the supply. Thus, in some cases, a giant medical system takes over as the only provider of major health-care services, limiting competition.

In a free market, patients should have information about the availability of health-care services as it promotes a better supply of services. However, in the United States, patients are not well informed about the decisions pertaining to the care they should receive. Thus, there is a huge information gap between consumers and available services. This gap can be filled with the help of the latest information management systems and the involvement of primary health-care personnel.

In a free market, patients can compare various service providers in terms of price and quality. Existing pricing systems confuse free market mechanisms, while hidden costs make it hard for patients to guess the full expenditure of rendered health services. It is ideal for health-care entrepreneurs when things are not in perfect shape as they can enter into the market with an effective solution to create that missing balance.

5. Government's Role as a Subsidiary to Private Sector

The government is a subsidiary of the private sector in the U.S. health-care system, whereas in other health-care systems the government runs it. In most developed countries, the government plays a central role in the provision of health care (e.g., the Veteran Affairs [VA] system in the United States). However, the private sector plays a dominant role because of American tradition and the desire to limit the government's role.

6. A Fusion of Market Justice and Social Justice

In the U.S. health-care system, there is a fusion of market justice and social justice. Social justice is necessary to deliver health-care services to everyone, but it is mitigated by market justice, which tries to help it find the right cost and improve utilization. Market justice places the responsibility for the fair distribution of health care on the market forces in a free economy.

Health care in the United States is a limited resource, so there has to be some way to distribute it. In market justice, market pressure is used to determine it. However, social justice emphasizes the well-being of the community over individuals.

In social justice, the community decides, instead of the market, how to ration out health care. Thus, if you are more of the market-justice-type person, you will see that interfering with market forces in a free economy. Also, it will be considered unjust as it will feel like you aren't justly distributing your health care. Further, the inability to obtain medical services because of a lack of financial resources will be considered unjust. In other words, having market pressure operates on whether a person's ability to get access to health care will be seen as unjust.

7. Several Key Players

There are many key players that create an unusual balance of power. Without the government as a central agency, everyone is fighting for a seat at the table, which leads to a quest for integration. The major players include

- physicians and all other providers,
- administrators of health-care institutions,
- insurance companies,
- large employers, and
- government.

In a nationalized health-care system in other developed countries, there are no physicians, administrators of health-care institutions, insurance companies, and large employers at the table. It is mainly the government having control with an absence of balance of power in the system.

These key players form different influential special interest groups according to their own economic interests. It becomes an issue when every group tries to work for its self-interest. For instance, health-care service providers try to maximize government compensations, while the government tries to contain increases in costs. Thus, conflict of interest arises, causing countering forces within the system.

8. Integration and Accountability

With all these players and in all these systems, this difficulty integrates to hold people and systems accountable for people's health. The envisioned role for primary care will include integrated health care by offering comprehensive, coordinated, and continuous services with seamless delivery. This emphasizes the importance of patient-provider relationships, especially with primary care providers, and how it can best function to improve the health of each individual while strengthening the population.

Integration and accountability are tough challenges. In the United States, there is a drive to utilize primary care as the organizing center for incessant and synchronized health-care services with seamless delivery. There is also a provider accountability system in the U.S. health-care system where providers have to provide quality health care efficiently and ethically. Thus, they cannot waste resources or withhold them. The patient accountability refers to a system in the U.S. health care where patients have to safeguard their own health and not to overuse resources but use them wisely.

9. Selective Access Based on Insurance Coverage

Access to health-care services is not universal in the United States as it is selectively based on insurance coverage. Workings are being done on this topic, but it still remains the case that a person has to have some sort of insurance coverage to get access to regular health-care services. Also, the providers are pressured by legal risks.

Other developed countries have national health-care programs to offer universal access. Theoretically, this leaves no citizen uninsured. The United States spends more per person on health care compared with other developed countries. Yet the system does not deliver commendable results. This is because a good share of the U.S. citizens do not have access to health-care services due to no or low insurance coverage.

10. Legal Risks

Because the U.S. health-care system has so much market justice involved with social justice and the government is not the leading player, legal risks influence practice behaviors. Because of the free market, providers take on legal risks when they deliver health care and are in constant competition. So when they offer a service having risk factors, they also have to have insurance against being sued.

This is the reason why private health-care providers fear being lured to court in a lawsuit for petty issues. To ensure their safety and to avoid any lawsuit activities, private health-care providers have set out additional tests with follow-up appointments to make sure they cover all requirements. But these unnecessary activities only elongate the medical procedures for patients with an extra cost, which they already are unable to afford. [21]

To conclude this chapter, I can say that the United States has a unique health-care system with its highs and lows, and it evidently lacks a universal access program. As a result, we can see that access to health-care services is not equally available to all U.S. citizens. Also, the whole system is not centrally aligned, whereas the private sector is more active and contributing compared with the government.

If we see it with a technological perspective, the system receives heavy investment and is more focused on technology-based solutions, which is a good point, I think. The information gap between consumers is also noticeable. The risk factors and legal concerns also make it difficult for providers to offer services at a low cost. I am sure you can see a few more characteristics as you reflect on it, and you must do so.

If we try to find a perfect health-care system, we may not find it anywhere across the globe. And this is why you can always find a window of opportunity in a health-care system not only in the United States but also anywhere in the whole world.

Though the health-care delivery system in the United States is unique, it lacks, to a certain extent, universal access. Hence, we can't say constant and all-inclusive health-care delivery is enjoyed by every U.S. citizen. The overall system is characterized by a patchwork of many subsystems that have been formed by market forces or the requirement of addressing a certain segment of the population. These subsystems include, for example, the military and VA systems, managed care, a system to address the needs of weak populations, and the evolving IDSs.

As you go through the health-care systems of various countries, you can find that there is no flawless health-care system anywhere in the world, and the United States is no exception. Many countries involve the private sector in their national health-care delivery systems to let things run smoothly, and the same thing is being done in the United States.

CHAPTER 3

Challenges and Opportunities for Health-Care Entrepreneurs

A lot of people have ideas, but there are few who decide to do something about them now. Not tomorrow. Not next week. But today. The true entrepreneur is a doer, not a dreamer.
—Nolan Bushnell

In spite of the massive size of the health-care market and the drive for innovation by entrepreneurs, the health-care industry is still in the first stages of its digital transition. It is true that entrepreneurs like Oscar Health and Theranos made headlines, though Theranos could not sustain itself. Still, there are many entrepreneurs who face hardships in making a dent in this multisided industry in which patients, providers, doctors, insurers, government institutions and regulators, and investors collide.

Coupled with the technology, the boom of health-care entrepreneurship is quite evident in this as well as the coming decades. Some who ventured in this industry thrived, and some dashed to the ground like HomeHero, Laguna Pharmaceuticals, and HealthSpot, among others. [22] Therefore, we may have many entrepreneurs out there who could be reluctant to commence their own health-care business. Thus, the challenges for health-care entrepreneurs could discourage a number of ambitious entrepreneurs from entering this fruitful market. In fact, the health-care sector is always in need of new ideas and efforts to improve the system. Here, one of the major means of improvement is the contribution of smart entrepreneurs.

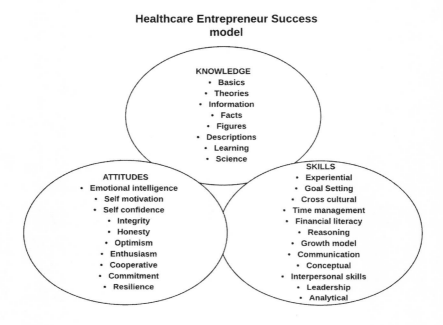

Healthcare Entrepreneur Success model

Figure 3.1

In the figure above, we can see the essential components of a health-care entrepreneur success model. The three major components are

- knowledge,
- attitudes, and
- skills.

Let me tell you one thing—an entrepreneur takes every challenge as a learning opportunity and has the ability to turn it into a golden chance. Therefore, the real challenge is your approach to dealing with the challenges in the industry. Being an entrepreneur is not about overnight success, but it demands patience, insight, and foresight to see and turn the challenges into golden opportunities.

Health care is a unique industry as it deals with people's health and well-being and is a matter of life and death of a human being; the legal challenges can turn really ugly in the case of mishaps. Therefore, successful entrepreneurs follow a methodical process to execute their plans as we have been following in this book so far. Previously, we understood the U.S. health-care system and its characteristics, and now we will focus on the challenges and opportunities in this chapter.

Trust

Trust is the most critical among all challenges; people's health is something no one can and should play around with it. The health-care entrepreneurs who go after money instead of trust fail miserably. As an entrepreneur, you need to keep in mind that consumers are highly cautious in the health-care sector compared with other industries; thus, they are highly sensitive about trust.

When you look at the past, you can see several scandals in health care, such as the case of "Pharma Bro" Martin Shkreli. [23] Immoral practices are widespread in several countries, and these scandals damage consumers' trust in the industry, especially in entrepreneurs. For instance, Theranos—a blood test technology firm—grew to the worth of $9 billion, but it could not prove the trustworthiness of its technology, which eventually led to the trial of Elizabeth Holmes and the ultimate closure of Theranos. [24]

Hence, earning and building trust is the first significant challenge for health-care entrepreneurs. If there is a challenge, there is always a way to overcome it. Thus, you can tackle this challenge with official recognition since people trust regulatory authorities such as FDA and FTC. You can attain certifications from these organizations, and there will be no reason for our target market to believe in your product or service.

Legal recognition will also help you be aware of wrong practices in the health business. A hindrance in the process is extended time to take all the approvals, and that is costly too; however, it is worth every second and cent.

Progress

You must have read stories about the swift growth of technology firms such as Google, Amazon, and Dropbox, among others. In the health-care sector, things are radically different. It may surprise you a bit, but the health-care sector is notorious for its slow growth. The reason is that every idea needs to go through a trial and error, and there is no possibility of launching anything untested; it is specifically true for a remedial rug or a device. Health care is all about people's well-being, so it may take months to years for a solution to be authenticated with scientific proof. Therefore, progress could be unforeseeable at times.

The world has not gotten rid of the coronavirus yet; the pandemic has already claimed almost four million lives across the world since January 2020. [25] In almost every developed country, scientists have been working hard to make the coronavirus vaccine, and vaccination of people has started in many countries. However, we never know how long it will take to wipe out this pandemic. Here, I can see a window of opportunity, but nobody can't just come up with a solution. In the context of slow progress, some entrepreneurs may not be able to survive within their very first years. Therefore, the overall budget and expenditures must be well calculated to prevent any surprises or disappointments later.

Irreplaceable Doctors

Another noticeable cause for slow growth and innovation is corporatism, which is rampant in the health-care sector. When the entire system is under fiscal pressure, corporatism turns out to be the ultimate obstacle that guards the interests of a particular party. We can see corporatism among doctors, especially the elite and powerful ones. Corporatism in the health-care sector is an archrival for innovation. As a result, entrepreneurs face obstacles when they attempt to apply ideas of radical innovation. It becomes even tougher if the entrepreneur is not a doctor himself. The manifestation of corporatism is felt more strongly due to stiff regulations. Moreover, politicians implement rules and regulations that are meant to target the competitors and new players, favoring particular parties.

Empowerment of the Patients

Since health is a sensitive matter of life and death, innovation seems to be slow. You can't conduct experiments with patients' lives. But the need for innovation is equally important since it is about saving precious human lives. At times, critical conditions demand more innovative ideas, whereas slowness can be more harmful. If you can find ways to empower patients, it will be a great contribution since the empowered patients can lead the charge. What I mean by empowered patients is that you need to come up with ideas that can help patients be proactive or an active part in the treatment process.

Rules and Regulations

Like a few other fields, health-care entrepreneurs are required to take certain permits before they can launch their product or service to their target market. It becomes more difficult with complicated rules as they grow their operations. Again, health care is a sensitive matter, so you will find no friction or exception in the rules. Moreover, corporatism plays its influencing part and takes all the advantage, making it hard for start-ups.

Competition

Since health care is a well-established sector, the competition is fierce while players are at various levels on the ground—some small, some big. There are renowned giants in diverse arenas like medicine and care with absolute dominance. In the presence of stiff competition, it is tough, indeed. For entrepreneurs, it could be like a battle between David and Goliath, and we know who the winner is. In the health-care industry, it is not about competing with the giants; it is about making a fortune by standing on the shoulders of giants. Thus, you are on the ground in the same team, not the opposing team, where you do not compete but cooperate. When you collaborate, you can find opportunities to revolutionize the sector with your innovative ideas. Merging with others could bring a mutual advantage.

Tech giants like Google and IBM have invested hugely in the health-care sector. Google's accelerator and incubator programs have already made investments in seventeen digital health firms that work in various areas that include genomics, clinical research, and insurance, among others. [26] Obviously, every start-up entrepreneur may not match their scope and vision in the early stages, so it will take some time. The ones who were spotted by these tech giants got investments in millions of dollars.

If you look around and notice, you can see that the health-care industry has many potential investors. It is up to you how strong your idea is and how you approach investors. Unquestionably, health care is a rich ground for entrepreneurs. To manage this challenge, you just need to make your competition your strength instead of creating competition.

Information Security and Privacy

Today medical institutions use technology to store patients' data. Electronic data storage is easy to manage, but it is always at risk like other technology-based databases. A data breach for exploitation can lead to disastrous consequences like blackmailing and loss of customers and finances, among others. Every health-care service is supposed to protect their patients' or clients' information, and this also builds trust. According to HIPAAJournal.com, "High numbers of healthcare records continue to be exposed each month. Across the 62 breaches, 2,583,117 healthcare records were exposed or compromised; however, it is below the 12-month average of 2,867,243 breached records per month. 34.4 million healthcare records have now been breached in the past 12 months, 11.2 million of which were breached in 2021." [27]

Lack of security can cause a downfall to any firm. So like other industries, information security is a prime concern for medical institutions, which makes this area appealing to health-care entrepreneurs.

Failure to Deliver the Promised Product/Service

Over-the-top claims are common among start-up entrepreneurs in various industries, but the health-care industry cannot forgive you for false claims. It is a serious industry in which the margin of error is dealt with zero tolerance. Failures are not new in this sector; in fact, some companies went down after successfully running for a decade or more.

Theranos was launched in 2003 and grew to reach $9 billion worth; however, it failed to prove the efficacy of its technology and was closed in 2018. The failure of Theranos is possibly the biggest one in this sector. You must have your health-care product or service go through the proper process of trial and error to prevent such a mishap.

Data-Driven Providers

Technology has already changed the way most business sectors collect data, whereas health care has more complications in collecting data for treatment and analysis since it is virtually endless. But the rigidity of hospitals and pharmaceutical make it complex to accept and integrate the digital economy in the system. Thus, we can observe a rift growing between what patients expect and what recognized players achieve pertaining to digital innovation and integration.

Digital innovation can also be an effective instrument for empowering patients. As we can witness the growth of digital innovation and means in the health-care industry, entrepreneurs have great opportunities in this particular area.

Health Insurance

Health care does not come free; in fact, sometimes it requires tons of money for the treatment of just one person and purchasing drugs. For instance, Zolgensma—manufactured by AveXis Inc.—is used in gene therapy for children less than two years old with spinal muscular atrophy. [28] The annual cost of Zolgensma is $2,125,000. [29] Evidently, Zolgensma is the most expensive drug ever. Thus, insurance companies come into play to offer coverage for health care. Since the insurance companies are involved in financials, they are among the most powerful players. For health insurers, data is the most valuable asset since it helps them determine the best candidates for their insurance policies.

Ecosystem

Understanding the health-care landscape is of utmost importance for entrepreneurs since it helps in spotting the gaps and opportunities in the whole system. By knowing the health care and your own ecosystem, you can create a complete road map to surefire success. Also, it will help you spot global opportunities as you do for digital entrepreneurship.

HIPAA Compliance

Meeting the rules and regulations of HIPAA is an essential task for health-care entrepreneurs. It will pose serious challenges later if you choose to ignore it in the beginning. According to Wikipedia: [30]

> The Health Insurance Portability and Accountability Act of 1996 (HIPAA or the Kennedy–Kassebaum Act) was enacted by the 104th United States Congress and signed by President Bill Clinton in 1996. It was created primarily

to modernize the flow of healthcare information, stipulate how personally identifiable information maintained by the healthcare and healthcare insurance industries should be protected from fraud and theft, and address limitations on healthcare insurance coverage.

The act consists of five titles. Title I of HIPAA protects health insurance coverage for workers and their families when they change or lose their jobs. Title II of HIPAA, known as the Administrative Simplification (AS) provisions, requires the establishment of national standards for electronic health care transactions and national identifiers for providers, health insurance plans, and employers. Title III sets guidelines for pre-tax medical spending accounts, Title IV sets guidelines for group health plans, and Title V governs company-owned life insurance policies.

Thus, the core purpose of HIPAA compliance is to keep the "confidentiality, integrity, and security" of electronic medical data, which has forty-two standard security rules regarding three groups (i.e., administrative, physical, and technical). As you deal with medical data, you must know who can access, edit, and delete data and how and where the data is being shared. Because of complications of HIPAA, it is a great challenge for entrepreneurs.

Telemedicine

Telemedicine refers to a digital platform that connects patients with doctors via telecommunication; thus, both parties remain at their own venues. Through telemedicine, doctors can diagnose, treat, and monitor patients remotely. [31] Telemedicine is not new; in fact, it has existed for four decades in the United States. It was chiefly used for rural communities to provide quick access to health-care professionals.

There are two kinds of telemedicine services, synchronous telehealth practice and asynchronous telemedicine practice. In synchronous telehealth practice, there is a two-way connection between doctors and patients. The main means for connection are video conference or a telemedicine app to simulate an in-person appointment. In asynchronous telemedicine practice, patient uploads his or her medical data via a telemedicine platform so that doctors can access it. Thus, there is no direct interaction between doctors and patients.

As technology is rising, we can see that the market and demand for telemedicine will grow exponentially. Since people are now busier and because of the recent lockdown due to the coronavirus pandemic, the need for telemedicine has gained momentum. Thus, telemedicine is a lucrative ground for health-care entrepreneurs to commence a venture in this rising industry.

Wearables

Wearable health-care technology refers to electronic devices that people can wear such as Fitbits and smart watches. These wearables are designed to collect a user's data pertaining to health and exercise. Among noticeable health-care wearables, we can see Ava (for tracking period cycles), AliveCor personal EKG (for taking medical-grade EKG recordings in thirty seconds), TempTraq (monitoring sensor for babies and children), Biopatch (for measuring patients' heart rate, ECG, heart rate variability, respiration rate, and activity), and many others. The demand for wearable technology has influenced the health-care industry, and it includes technology firms and even insurance companies. [32]

This industry is promising and on the rise with lots of room to cover in the coming days. According to Business Insider Intelligence research, the number of health and fitness trackers and wearables in the United States will grow at a 10 percent annual rate by 2023. [33] This rise will also be influential on the decisions of insurance firms and health-care providers. Thus, there are explicit opportunities for health-care entrepreneurs.

Social Media

As technology is advancing, communication channels have also become quick, and social media seems to make it even quicker and easier. Today health-care services and professionals utilize online social networks to contact, interact, and grow their relationship with their patients. Also, social media helps in launching public awareness campaigns. Doctors and patients are on social media bandwagon; it has become a popular trend, and it is going to stay there for a long time to come. When health-care professionals, patients, and other relevant services and companies are there, health-care entrepreneurs can surely see some great opportunities on social media.

New Players Are Empowered and Fearless

Today's youth is empowered by technology and data, so they have this innate capability to spot and create new opportunities. The health-care industry is lucrative enough to draw the attention of entrepreneurial talent even from other fields, especially digital ones. This young lot of talent has the capacity to resolve the hardest issues in the industry.

The best thing about technology is that it has brought together the top-tier thinkers from multiple fields on the same table, be it data science, business, or finance. Thus, there is a great potential for investment and backing for new players from the industry giants like venture capitalists and veteran corporate leaders.

In every industry, entrepreneurs face various challenges, and health care is no exception. The good news is that these challenges open up many windows of opportunities for visionary entrepreneurs. Today huge corporates and investors are ready to invest in the health-care sector. Thus, health-care entrepreneurs can expand at a fast speed and beat all the odds by turning them into golden opportunities. As it is coupled with revolutionary technology, our era can be considered a golden era for health-care entrepreneurship. There are challenges and equal opportunities for visionaries in this sector.

Paperwork and Administrative Burdens

The health-care industry is overregulated, which causes paperwork and administrative burdens on the health-care service providers. In the 2018 *Medical Economics* Physician Report, 79 percent of doctors considered paperwork and administrative burdens the topmost challenge. According to Kevin Riddleberger, a cofounder and chief strategy officer at DispatchHealth, "Paperwork or administrative duties is not the best use of clinicians' time and resources, and directly impacts patient care and increases physician burnout."

Kyle Varner, an internist at the Tripler Army Medical Center, shares his concerns that he has to spend more time on his computer to document the patients' information than he does with his patients. Mr. Varner states, "This is not because I am trying to create a good record of the care—it is because I have to play semantic games so that the hospital gets paid." In short, the health-care industry is overregulated, and it could be a tough task to cater to each and every clause and condition for health-care entrepreneurs. [34]

Ever-Rising Overhead Cost

U.S. health care is one of the most expensive systems. [35] A report from the AMA stated, "The United States spent $3,795.4 billion on health care in 2019." [36] The Centers for Medicare and Medicaid Services estimates that the national health expenditures will rise to $6 trillion by the year 2027. [37] The possible reasons include the aging population, chronic disease prevalence, rising drug prices, and health-care service and administrative costs. This factor can seriously affect your pricing strategy. [38]

Understanding and Transitioning to Value-Based Care Philosophy

According to NEJM Catalyst:

> Value-based healthcare is a healthcare delivery model in which providers, including hospitals and physicians, are paid based on patient health outcomes. Under value-based care agreements, providers are rewarded for helping patients improve their health, reduce the effects and incidence of chronic disease, and live healthier lives in an evidence-based way. Value-based care differs from a fee-for-service or capitated approach, in which providers are paid based on the amount of healthcare services they deliver. The "value" in value-based healthcare is derived from measuring health outcomes against the cost of delivering the outcomes. [39]

The philosophy of value-based care sounds good, but it has its own challenges to face, such as lack of system integration, outdated practice workflows, inadequate inside resources, trouble in getting buy-in, siloed health-care delivery, inaccessibility of clinical data, and high monetary risk, among others. [40]

Hiring and Retaining Competent Staff

Hiring is an essential job when a health-care start-up is launched. And the right hiring is mandatory to steer in the right direction. Over time as the company grows, the hiring continues, and many new challenges arise regarding the retention of staff members, especially the competent ones.

Cost of Electronic Health Record System

The implementation and management cost of an electronic health record system involves direct and indirect expenditures. Typically, an EHR system costs around $162,000 annually, with a maintenance cost of $85,000 from the next year. Also, training cost is required at times when there is an addition of new members in staff or when there is an update in the overall system. [41]

Legal Liabilities

In the health-care business, there are certain risks since it is a matter of life and death. Thus, as a health-care entrepreneur, you need to consider each and every aspect of legal liabilities beforehand instead of waiting for the disaster to happen. If you are in the technology sector of health care, still, things can go awry, so don't leave anything to guesswork.

With a perfectly designed health-care business model, you also need to be well prepared to launch and sell it. In fact, the sales cycle could be a bit longer in this sector, depending on your product or service, especially when it comes to selling technology-based products. Thus, the health-care sector is a challenging area for entrepreneurs. And this is why there are more opportunities for entrepreneurs, especially for those who are working for a technology-driven solution. Thus, it is safe to say that health-care entrepreneurship is worth your effort.

CHAPTER 4

Starting a Health-Care Business

Good business leaders create a vision, articulate the vision, passionately own the vision, and relentlessly drive it to completion.

—Jack Welch

Since you have decided to start your own business, it is necessary to know everything related to the types of health-care services and commercial companies. This way, you can determine which service and type of company will best suit your needs. Once you know it all as a health-care entrepreneur, you can decide to launch your business venture in the most appropriate way possible. The fact of creating a company does not mean that you will stop being autonomous, but what varies when you do is the services, size, and legal status of your health-care business and the obligations that you must comply with.

Types of Health-Care Services

For entrepreneurs, health care is a vast field with lots of opportunities to start their venture. Again, it is about gaining the right knowledge at the right time. Let's see some of the areas you can consider to start your own health-care business.

Inpatient Care

According to the Health Services Act, inpatient care as health care cannot be provided on an outpatient basis. Thus, it must be provided in a health-care facility with twenty-four-hour operating hours. Inpatient care activities include diagnostic, therapeutic, and rehabilitation care. Inpatient care ensures continuity of comprehensive care to the patient once he or she has passed the possibilities of primary care and in coordination with it.

It is provided according to the characteristics of the patient and process during hospital admission. Patient access to hospital emergency care is provided twenty-four hours a day to those suffering from an acute clinical situation that requires immediate attention. Inpatient service is carried out by referral from the primary care physician or specialized or for reasons of urgency or vital risk that may require exclusive therapeutic measures of the hospital environment. There are four types of inpatient care:

- Acute standard inpatient care
- Acute intensive inpatient care
- Follow-up inpatient care
- Long-term inpatient care

1. Acute Standard Inpatient Care

Acute standard inpatient care is provided in the following situations:

- Sudden illness
- Sudden and threatening deterioration of the chronic condition
- Inevitable inpatient performance of a medical procedure
- To begin a medical rehabilitation program

2. Acute Intensive Inpatient Care

Acute intensive inpatient care is provided in the following situations:

- A sudden bodily malfunction
- A sudden threat to basic bodily functions
- Indication for bodily malfunction

3. Follow-Up Inpatient Care

Follow-up inpatient care is provided in the following situations:

- Patients with a baseline diagnosis who are in stable condition now
- Patients with a sudden illness or deterioration of a chronic illness
- Patients who need follow-up or therapeutic, rehabilitative care
- Patients dependent on (partially or totally) vital bodily function support

4. Long-Term Inpatient Care

Long-term inpatient care is provided in the following situations:

- Patients whose health shows improvement by prescribed medical treatments
- Patients who need continuing provision of nursing care to stay in a stable condition
- Patients with impaired basic bodily function

Preventive Care

Preventive care refers to the type of routine care that includes screening services. Preventive care is aimed at regular medical checkups and medical advice to help people improve their health, prevent disease, and improve care for existing conditions. A primary care doctor carries out preventive examinations and prescribes vaccinations against infectious diseases.

Some more area to consider include the following:

- Medical rescue service and emergency service
- Occupation and work-related medical services
- Dispensary care
- Spa therapeutic and rehabilitative care
- Provision of medicines
- Provision of medical devices and gears [42]

Health care is a massive industry with a lot of innovative business opportunities. Some of the platforms offering such lucrative opportunities are as follows:

- Health-related mobile application and website marketing
- Online pharmacy
- Medical transcription services
- Medical and hospital equipment distribution
- Yoga studio
- Chemist and druggist stores
- Diagnostic center
- Elderly care services
- Substance addiction amenities
- MRI scanning services
- Virtual doctor services
- Private ambulance services
- Medical health insurance selling
- Health management consulting [43]
- Medical transcription services
- Medical records management
- Physical/occupational therapy center
- Health-care app
- Diabetic care center
- Home health-care service
- Medical foot care
- Drug treatment/rehabilitation center
- Childbirth services
- Medical billing service
- Nutritionist/dietitian
- Alternative health care
- Health information website
- Medical supply sales
- Stylish uniforms for medical professionals
- Hearing aid dispensary
- Respite care service for caregivers
- Medical marijuana dispensary
- Spas and massage saloons [44]

Types of Business Entities

Now dedicate time to studying the type of commercial companies that exist to be able to select the one that could best suit your needs. Here, it is necessary to take into account the number of people or partners who make up the business, the responsibility that is required of each of the partners, and the initial capital for the business.

Any profession, based on a group of people who work on the basis of a series of agreements, is developed through commercial companies or organizations through a legal form acquired by involved entities, constituted with a certain capital in which several partners participate. The types of commercial companies will be determined depending on the activity to which the company is dedicated. Since selling a product and offering a service are not the same, just like a vehicle is different from a shirt or a plane ticket from an airplane, it is necessary to study and analyze the different factors comprehensively to determine the type of health-care company you want to create.

Thus, a commercial company is a union or agreement between two or more people who have a defined capital that is based on the objectives or the economic activity that the company wants to give. There must be a contractual consensus to defend the obligations and rights of each of the partners. The company can be set in an activity that carries benefits and objectives that can be disparate to become a commercial company.

For legal purposes, a legal citizen in a country can establish a company, that is, any person who has rights and obligations and has the legal capacity to establish a company. It is necessary to be clear about the difference between a partnership and sole business. The law does not contemplate any type of special requirement for a person to start their business activity; it is only required that they have a legal capacity, which means that they do not have any type of legal impediment by the judgment of a court.

You need to consider the following characteristics when you create your health-care company:

1. The number of partners who will participate in your project
2. The initial capital with which you will start your business
3. People responsible for the product manufacturing or service provision

Starting from these three characteristics, you can classify the most suitable type of commercial company for you among the ones mentioned below.

The types of companies are divided into the following categories depending on the following:

- Nature
- Constitution
- Commercial activity
- Origin of capital

According to the characteristics of the company, they are classified as

- degree of participation in the market,
- level of contribution to the state such as taxes,
- level of contribution to society (i.e., employment opportunities), and
- competitiveness level.

Types of Companies According to Legal Nature

Microenterprises

Microenterprises are made up of no more than ten employees, and they are generally registered as the property of a single employer or shareholders. They are characterized as such because the owner is part of the group of employees, and his or her participation in the market is minimal since the work and manufacture are commonly rudimentary or handmade. [45]

According to Data.OECD.org:

Small and medium-sized enterprises (SMEs) employ fewer than 250 people. SMEs are further subdivided into micro enterprises (fewer than 10 employees), small enterprises (10 to 49 employees), medium-sized enterprises (50 to 249 employees). Large enterprises employ 250 or more people. [46]

Small- and medium-sized enterprises (SMEs) are the heart of the market for their entrepreneurial spirit. They are characterized by limited resources and low capital, but they are often very profitable and independent.

Large enterprises are characterized by offices, machinery, and industrialized manufacturing. They are usually listed on the stock market, depending on the product. They have shareholders, partners, and significant influence within the market.

Types of Companies According to Commercial Activity

They are divided according to their participation in the production system.

Primary Sector

They are the basis of the production of any company because their function is the extraction of natural goods such as agriculture, livestock, oil, minerals, and so on.

Secondary Sector

They process the material extracted by companies in the primary sector to later offer it to the market for the tertiary sector. They have the machinery and elements necessary to transform the raw material.

Tertiary Sector

They have the human talent necessary to perform the physical or intellectual tasks necessary for the product or service to reach consumers.

Types of Companies According to the Origin of Capital

They are divided according to their source of capital generation.

Public Companies

They are financed by the state, and their objective varies according to the target audience, be it citizens or the international market.

Private Companies

Its capital comes from individuals' private resources.

Mixed Companies

They work with state and private capital, creating an association of shared goods.

Types of Companies According to Territorial Scope

Depending on the territorial scope of their activity, these companies can be divided into the following:

Local

They have a limited scope and are generally micro-, small, or medium-sized companies.

Regional

They operate in a specific region, such as a state or province.

National

They operate throughout the country, which usually implies a highly specialized economic and commercial structure. Large companies respond to this model, although a micro-, small, or medium-sized company with the capacity to supply a national demand can also fall into this category.

International

They operate inside and outside the country. They have the greatest reach since they can offer their products or services in different markets.

Types of Companies According to the Legal Constitution

Each company is unique and has its own characteristics, but the Treasury cannot make a plan for each one of them. This is why the legal requirements, documents of incorporation, and collection of taxes depend on the type of company according to its legal constitution.

Sole Proprietorships (Schedule C Business)

A sole proprietorship is a company undertaken by a single person who has the necessary characteristics to carry out the management of a business. It allows its owner to carry out various commercial activities as established in the law. After a sole proprietorship is registered in the constitution, it becomes recognized as a legal entity, in this case sole proprietorship, because it is owned by a single owner. To register a sole proprietorship, the owners must have the name of the company with an identity document that identifies the new company to be registered, and it must contain the domicile and address of the owner of the company.

Sole proprietorships allow entrepreneurs to direct a large part of their assets to the creation of certain businesses, offering them legal status and making their responsibilities limited to the amount assigned to the new company. In addition, the employer can advance without having other people to collaborate as if they are partners. [47]

Pros

- The owner has the necessary legal elements in his or her favor to create a company that is supported by the law.
- It allows entrepreneurs to create a new legal personality to protect themselves from liabilities.
- The entrepreneur may carry on doing business as a natural person even if the company declares bankruptcy; thus, the owner's name will not be at risk, only the legal name that he or she creates with the new company.
- The entrepreneurs can protect their patrimony from the responsibilities of the new company only by putting at risk the capital of the investment to start the company.

Cons

- The owner is completely accountable for everything that takes place in the company. If there are debts, they will affect the owner's personal assets, such as home, savings, and other assets.
- Taxes applied are based on self-employment to sole proprietorships.
- The business ends with the owner's death or departure since the business and the owner are one.
- It is difficult to raise capital, so the initial funds are generated by the owners. [48]

Limited Liability Company (LLC)

A limited liability company (LLC) is formed when your intention is to form a health-care company with other partners, who will also make decisions and will be responsible for capital contributions both in goods and in a monetary way. Generally, this type of company requires a minimum contribution of capital for creation. LLC is a very common type of partnership among small businesses. [49]

Pros

- The liability to creditors is limited to the amount of capital stock.
- The procedure is much simpler.
- The incorporation costs are reasonable.
- The minimum capital required is relatively low.
- It does not have a minimum number of partners, so it can be made up of a single person.
- There is the flexibility of being taxed as a sole proprietor, partnership, S corporation, or C corporation.
- It has less paperwork.
- The filing costs are lower.

Cons

- An LLC member cannot pay wages to himself or herself.
- Depending on the state, renewal fees or publication requirements can be costly.

- Some states have a franchise or capital values tax on LLCs.
- There could be more partners, so you have to take everybody in confidence before every decision. [50]

LLCs Taxed as Partnerships

It is by default that an LLC that has more than one member is taxed as a partnership and has to pay taxes per the governing partnership tax rules and regulations. The partners need to fill Form 1065 and provide Schedule K-1, along with their personal tax returns. It is not necessary for the LLC to pay taxes directly. Instead, all partners can report their income and losses and pay taxes according to their share.

LLC Taxed as a C Corporation

Generally speaking, LLCs prefer to be taxed as C corporations for saving their taxes. The members act as shareholders instead of being self-employed. The corporate tax rate may be lower compared with the tax rates for personal income.

LLC Taxed as an S Corporation

The LLC members can divide income from the S corporation as an employee. The S corporation owners who work as an employee are paid reasonable salaries and have to pay FICA tax on their salaries. Since the S corporation profits are distributed to owners, it prevents double taxation.

Single-Member LLC (SMLLC) as Disregarded Entities

A disregarded entity refers to single-member LLCs, which suggests that the LLC is "ignored" for federal tax purposes. Thus, the IRS treats SMLLCs and their owner as the same person. By the way, it is only for federal taxes. As for the legal side, the SMLLC and the owner remain separate, whereas the LLC protects the owner's personal assets. An SMLLC for the IRS is ignored and nonexistent, and the LLC and the owner are the same. Thus, it signifies that the LLC is not a separate entity. If the SMLLC owner does not elect to be taxed as a corporation, it is considered a disregarded entity by default.

- In the case of a single LLC owner, Form 1040 is used to show incomes and losses.
- In the case of a corporation as owner, Form 1120 is used to show incomes and losses and Form 1120S for S corporation.

Partnership

A partnership is a company with more than one owner. When you decide to start a company with one or more people, you automatically enter into a partnership agreement. Partnerships are legal business entities that are registered with the state and can legally give limited liability protection to guard their assets.

Just like a sole proprietorship, a partnership is also legally and financially attached to the owners. Profits, losses, debts, and liabilities pass to all owners' personal income for tax. A partnership-based company is easier and less expensive compared with corporations.

Pros

- It is less formal, whereas legal obligations are fewer.
- It is easy to start a partnership business since partners can form it verbally or in writing.
- There are more people on board to share the overall burden and give advice.
- Since there are more people involved, there is more knowledge, skills, and experience collectively.
- All partners can brainstorm and make better decisions.
- There is no obligation to share the business affairs and any documents to the public.
- Raising high capital becomes easier.
- There is room to include more partners for the company's growth.

Cons

- The partners' liability regarding business debts is unlimited. Thus, every partner is jointly and severally liable for the partnership's debts.
- The risk of disagreements and friction is possible.

- Every partner is accountable for other partners' doings.
- When a partner departs, revaluing partnership assets costs expensive.

General Partnership (GP)

General partnership refers to a business owned by two or more people with an agreement to administer the business as co-owners. Unless otherwise agreed, all partners are entitled to receive an equal share of profit and loss. All partners manage the business and undertake responsibilities for the partnership's debts. When the agreement is created, you must clearly define the plan on selling or closing the business in case of partnership dissolution.

Since the company is not separate from its partners, profits are taxed at the personal income level instead of at the company level. GPs are easy to found, low-cost, and flexible. However, the personal assets of all partners remain at risk since all partners are legally responsible for one another's actions.

Limited Partnership (LP)

Limited partnerships have more defined structures and also carry the characteristics of a general partnership. To begin a company under a limited partnership, at least one general and one limited partner are required. Limited partners are investors and may not be a part of decision-making. Also, their risks and responsibilities are lesser than a general partner. If they start getting involved in business matters, they can lose the assigned status. Unlike limited partners, general partners are fully involved in the business operations; thus, they have more control, responsibilities, rights, and liabilities in a limited partnership.

Limited Liability Partnership (LLP)

In a limited liability partnership, business owners don't have personal liability for the debts of the business and their partners' doings. In the case of a legal action against the business, owners are not accountable in their personal capacity. New partners can be added or removed easily in LLPs. [51]

S Corporation (S Corp)

This type of entity is a corporation that has elected to be treated as an S corporation; *S* is for "small." This choice can be made by all those corporations that meet a series of requirements, including that they have less than one hundred shareholders and that they are U.S. citizens or residents. In the United States, a corporation may elect to be treated for tax purposes as an S corporation. This allows small businesses to enjoy the benefits of being legally treated as a corporation while avoiding double taxation.

For the purposes of the IRS, the taxes of an S corp are similar to those of partnerships. As in partnerships, the income, deductions, and tax credits of an S corporation are passed on to shareholders annually. Therefore, earnings are taxed at the shareholder level and not at the corporate level. The typical characteristics of the S corp are as follows:

- The owners/shareholders file an informative tax return.
- They do not pay taxes directly; the obligation to pay the tax falls on the shareholders.
- They have limited liability.
- Active partners are under the obligation to have a reasonable salary.
- If the partners meet the requirement of having a salary, they are not obliged to pay the self-employment tax.

Pros

- The corporation's losses pass directly to the shareholders and can be used to lower taxes on other income.
- Capital gains or exempt income is passed on directly to shareholders.
- Tax credits are passed on proportionally to the partners.
- Owners' personal assets are protected in case of any problems with finances and taxes.
- The ownership can be transferred easily.

Cons

- The formation is tricky in terms of legalities.
- There are a few stock restrictions due to liability and pass-through laws.

- Tax obligations and the IRS are very strict.
- There is little flexibility in reallocating incomes and losses. [52]

C Corporation (C Corp)

A C corporation is a legal entity with its own legal personality, commonly known as a corporation. It has a separate life from its owners and also its own rights and responsibilities. The notable characteristics of the C corporation are as follows:

- You must register with the state where the operations will be carried out.
- The life of the corporation is perpetual.
- It can be owned by one or more shareholders.
- Shareholders have limited liability, so they are not responsible for their personal assets for business obligations.
- The administrators, managers, or members of the board of directors of a corporation may or may not be shareholders.
- It has an obligation to declare and pay the taxes that correspond to the profit obtained.
- The shareholders, in turn, must pay taxes on the dividends they receive from the corporation.
- It does not pass on losses earned to the shareholders.

Pros

- The corporation obtains a legal personality (i.e., it is a "person" with a new life, with rights and obligations). In cases of litigation for any corporate management, the corporation will be sued, not its owners in their personal character.
- In tax terms, C corporations have the right to deduct expenses and payments for their administration and depreciation of personal property. In addition, they may obtain tax exemptions if they meet the requirements of the applicable law.
- The transfer or sale of shares is easy.

Cons

- A corporation cannot claim the constitutional rights that natural persons possess (i.e., the right to defend itself in court, the right to claim protection over privileges and immunities, and the right to non-self-incrimination).
- In tax terms, the corporation will pay for the income obtained from its operations, and the owners will also pay in their personal capacity for the dividends obtained in the commercial management of what they participate in. [53]

Professional Corporation

A professional corporation is another form of the corporation for people who offer professional services like doctors, consultants, and lawyers. These professionals are treated as small businesses by the IRS with reference to the tax code. A professional corporation can be either a sole proprietorship or a partnership, whereas they are treated with the same tax rules. The owners also function as employees.

Pros

- The owners can get tax breaks, which are unavailable for unincorporated businesses, such as retirement plans and 401(k) plans.
- They can provide tax-free health and life insurance via the Voluntary Employees' Beneficiary Association (VEBA).
- They can offer tax deductions and other fringe benefits for employees.
- Being tax-free can continue in case a shareholder dies or departs.

Cons

- If there is a loss in business, passive loss limitations limit the amount that nonactive shareholders can deduct for tax purposes.
- Partners can deduct their share of loss from personal taxable income.
- They have a flat corporate tax rate. [54]

How to Start a Health-Care Business

When you want to start your own health-care business, you must first define what your market is, to whom your product or service is going to be directed. For that, you must know what the needs of consumers are and what they want. Once you have that information, you can use it to create a marketing campaign. Through market research, valuable information is obtained about the tastes of customers and what they want to find in their favorite brand.

You must have generated a great health-care business idea, but nothing will work properly and smoothly until you have created a clear road map to launch and run your business along with dealing the legal matters. Thus, before undertaking anything, you have a great tool called a feasibility plan to measure the success of your health-care company. Let's see what a feasibility plan is and what components it has.

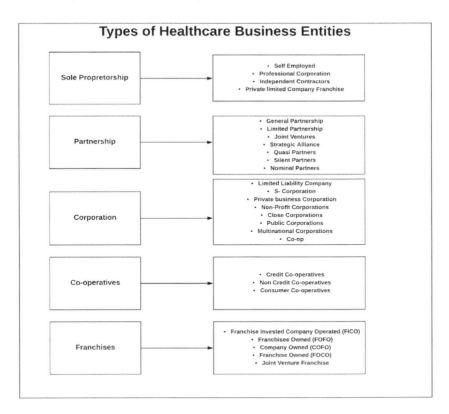

Figure 4.1

Feasibility Plan

The feasibility plan is a document that allows planning, controlling, and evaluating of the economic profitability of a business project, from the most basic points to the details of the launch. In short, it is the document that defines to third parties if your business idea is economically and commercially viable or not.

The content of the feasibility plan depends absolutely on the activity of the company. A perfect feasibility plan may not exist, nor is there a script or canon for the absolute success of the plan. However, I can give you the necessary points to create one from scratch. No matter how small the business idea is, I recommend that you make a feasibility plan, even if it is short, so that you can define the variables and the aspects to take into account, have a list of everything you need, define how you are going to do it and sell it, and establish what you want to achieve with your health-care business.

Components of a Feasibility Plan

You must define the following business ideas:

- **The business idea:** What product or service do you want to offer?
- **The operations plan:** How will you make the product or service, and how much does it cost to do it?
- **The marketing plan:** How are you going to sell the product or service?
- **The financial plan:** What financial means are necessary?
- **Legal procedures:** What laws and conditions do you need to launch your business idea?

To make the process easy, first, ask yourself the following questions:

For business idea

- What are the main characteristics of your health-care business idea?
- Is the idea interesting and profitable?
- What resources do you need to put your idea into practice?

- How will you present your idea?
- What exactly will you offer?
- What is the name of the business?
- Where will the company be located? Why?
- How should you write the business idea of your viability plan?

For market research

- Are there potential clients?
- What are their demographics?
- Do you have contacts with potential clients?
- Are there other companies that carry out the same activity?
- What does the competition offer? How and at what price?

To do an easy market study for your feasibility plan, you can calculate the number of inhabitants in the area of presence of the company (demographic censuses) multiplied by the rate of users in the activity, which will be equal to your potential customers.

For the operations plan

- What are the phases of the production process?
- What are the properties of your business premises (surface, cost, payment, characteristics, etc.)?
- What furniture do you need (equipment, materials, software, machinery)?
- What and how much raw material and supplies do you need?
- What providers do you need? What will be the payment terms?
- What and how much staff do you need for your company? Make a detailed description of each position, type of contract, form of payment, and so on.
- What is the distribution of each employee's responsibility?
- Will you need means of transportation? Which?
- What security measures do you need to establish?
- Will you take out any insurance against theft, fire, damage, and so on?

For the marketing plan

- What product or service are you going to offer?
- At what price will you offer your product or service?
- What name will you put to the product or service?
- What system will you use to control the quality of the product or service?
- How will you sell? How will you get paid?
- What are the distribution channels for your product or service?
- What will be the means of promoting the product (digital marketing, i.e., social networks and search engines, traditional advertising, content marketing, etc.)?

For financial plan

- In the first place, what financial resources do you have?
- Do you need any type of loan? If yes, on what conditions?
- Are you entitled to any public/private subsidy?
- Will you outsource to carry out your product or service?
- What must be the volume of sales per month so that the business is profitable, and when will you reach it?

For legal procedures

- What are the laws that benefit your business?
- What are the laws that sanction your business?
- What are the requirements, conditions, procedures, and paperwork to launch the product or service, the company, the premises, the machinery, the transport, the suppliers, employees, and so on?
- What are the requirements of registration in all relevant bodies?
- What are the political, economic, social, and environmental obligations of your company?
- What are the privacy policies, conditions of use, copyright, trademark, and so on? [55]

Growth

This shows a hypothesis of how potential audience will know the product, how you propose to solve distribution problems, and some possible forms of advertising.

Maturity

Once the product is established and the customers are stable, you must plan how you will act to keep it that way and reward your customers. The longer this stage lasts, the better and greater the benefits.

Decline

If the product or service has been saturated or the customers abandon the product for your competition, you must plan or foresee action strategies to counteract this issue. This is the most dangerous stage, and it is usually very fast. Onset is not detected, and usually, when they are detected, it is too late. Above all, to counteract this, you must stay informed and updated and continue to innovate your product or service.

A feasibility plan helps you see the overall road map of your business. Now it is time to get in more details of all sections of the feasibility plan, starting with an effective good business plan. This way, you can determine if your idea is worth the investment.

Business Plan

When health-care entrepreneurs decide to start their business idea, they persevere with passion and creativity until they succeed. And you can do it too, and I don't have doubts. Therefore, the business plan is the most recommended before you crystallize your project. With this effective tool, you will be able to plan and execute a series of strategies and see if it is possible to specify and achieve your objectives.

A business plan is a document in which you must present the planning and execution of the entire process of your health-care business. The business plan will involve questions, answers, and explanations of everything. By doing so, you will be able to improve, correct, and verify important aspects that, in one way or another, can positively or negatively influence your idea.

Is It Complicated to Make a Business Plan?

This is the typical question that many investors ask. But remember, for a good entrepreneur, obstacles do not exist, or they are minimized. However, my answer is *no*. It is not complicated at all. On the contrary, it is easy because it is about presenting information that you know and that you master about your goods or services. In short, it is about the business you are creating.

Since it is your business with its own characteristics, no business plan will be or will resemble yours. Each one is original and unique, with a purpose and an established strategy. It is the guide that presents the strategic route to follow so that your business idea can become a reality, so it is not difficult at all. In short, it is an objective and organized way to start and develop a commercial health-care business project.

A business plan helps you establish goals and objectives that are within reach of the capabilities of each investor. Although problems and obstacles arise, what will lead you to success is your effort, perseverance, passion, creativity, and determination.

Explain Your Business Objectives

It is an executive summary, so you need to provide all the data on the activities that your company will develop (i.e., name, mission, vision, values, and all aspects related to your business profile).

Define the Problem

It is about presenting in detail the problem you want to solve. So make a list of the obstacles that your company will solve for its customers with its product or service. You can include examples that explain how this process will be carried out. In short, determine the situation you want to solve.

Clarify the Solution

You must explain how your company is going to solve the identified problems, the business opportunity it represents, and the strategies you will develop to achieve the objectives proposed at this point.

Tell Your Story

Explain your initiative to create your business idea so your work team and your clients can know the origins of this venture that aims to be special and unique, in addition to satisfying the needs and wishes of customers.

Describe Your Audience

Describe what your potential customers, your current customers, and your target and key audience are like. Make a market segmentation and classify them by groups so that you can determine the campaigns for each one.

Define Your Competition

Name your competition and point out their main qualities. Establish points of differentiation and how they are alike. Define how they behave, where they are, and what their prices are. Also, include the advantageous qualities of your business over the competition.

Explain Your Product or Service

Describe the product or service you will market and explain the possible development plan. It is also necessary to clarify what tools will be used to achieve this.

Select the Organizational Model of Your Company

In this step, you need to define three main aspects:
- How will the price of your product or service and the profit margin be set?
- How are you going to sell and distribute your product or service?
- How do you plan to advertise your company and product or service?

Present Your Entrepreneurial Team

Describe the members of your work team. Explain the skills, functions, experiences, and qualities of each of them and assign responsibilities with their respective curricula vitae and the type of project you are involved in. Moreover, you have to incorporate the required positions, the needs of the staff, and the human resources policy.

Financial Forecast

Explain and predict the monthly or yearly profit margin and monthly business expenses. In addition to presenting all the fundamental financial information, explain cash flow, profit margin, billing, taxes, and things in a similar vein.

I know that developing a business plan is a long process, but it is worth it. It is the beginning of your dream that will come true, so don't miss the opportunities you must undertake and work with perseverance until you achieve your goals. Be ready to discover your entrepreneurial potential.

Marketing Plan

One of the pillars of a company is its marketing plan. For each product, service, brand, or person, it is completely different, so you need to design just the one your health-care business needs. A marketing plan is to look for the strategies under which you can enter the market. Every entrepreneur needs to visualize how the business launch will be. To ensure an organized brainstorming, you need to clearly define the mission that the said marketing plan will fulfill (i.e., attracting customers and promoting business).

Marketing Plan Objectives

They should be clear, specific, and practical and state what and when the actions should be carried out. In this way, you will be able to determine if the proposed marketing strategies are effective. Despite the fact that a new business is always full of illusions for a successful marketing plan, it is necessary to quantify each action and result.

Market Analysis

Starting with the marketing plan, you must know the current market situation, the position of competitors within it, and how your product or service will influence. Take into account the presence of the public within social networks. Quantify user interactions with content similar to that of your company and the content of the competition; in this way, you will know what they like the most and how and when they want it.

SWOT

SWOT stands for 'strengths, weaknesses, opportunities, and threats.' SWOT identifies an analysis matrix that allows diagnosing the strategic situation in which a company, organization, institution, or person finds itself to carry out a successful project. It was developed at the Stanford Research Institute, United States, between 1960 and 1970 with the collaboration of M. Dosher, Dr. O. Benepe, A. Humphrey, Birger Lie, and R. Stewart. The success of this tool in the business environment made it soon be implemented in other areas.

The study of the SWOT matrix allows us to identify problems, foresee scenarios, predict complications, find solutions, visualize weak points of the entity, and transform them into strengths and opportunities. A rigorous analysis of the data collected allows the formulation and selection of the strategies to be followed. It allows us to analyze all the elements that involve a business or project to meet the set objectives.

Strengths and Weaknesses

It is about identifying the strengths and weaknesses of an entity, a crucial step to know which human, material, and environmental resources can be counted on in a concrete way (strengths) and which ones are missing or should be strengthened (weaknesses).

Opportunities and Threats

Once the strengths and weaknesses have been identified, it is necessary to identify the opportunities and threats, that is, favorable (opportunities) or unfavorable (threats) circumstances, for further development of the project in question. For example, what are the environmental conditions (close collaborators or competitors, clients, demographics, political conditions, environmental conditions, laws, etc.), and what may be the interest groups for or against (governments, unions, institutions, communities, and shareholders)? [56]

Target Audience and Real Customers

Although it is hard to believe, a few are lucky enough that their real clients meet the perfect profile of the target audience, but it is not a bad thing that it does not happen since it will give you a more realistic and segmented vision of the market. Creating a consumer profile based on the needs that they must have to purchase the product or service can be somewhat complicated, which is why market tests fit perfectly here. You can conduct surveys through various social networks. For example, Facebook has very effective tools for this. If it is a product, I recommend that you put together a small group with varied personalities and give them a taste of your product.

The important thing for the marketing plan is the data as it will help you monitor the performance of the strategy. In this way, you will perfect your plan as your company grows. The launch stage is essential for data collection; ask your real customers if they would like to fill out a survey about your product, and you will know why they chose it.

Marketing Objectives

The marketing objectives can be divided into quantitative and qualitative categories.

Quantitative Objectives

They provide figures to perform statistics based on a need, question, or idea.

- Increase number of clients
- Generate greater receptivity of content on social networks
- Increase the number of registered users

Qualitative Objectives

By their nature, they are impossible to quantify, but their study is carried out through observation and analysis.

- Improve customer service
- Increase brand popularity
- Position the product within the market
- Identify strategies, tactics, and promotion

In this phase, a good public relations plan, advertising campaigns, or visual strategies of the product come into play. For tools, you can employ advertising banners on specific pages or promotional campaigns within social networks. I also recommend that you keep a calendar of objectives; in this way, you will ensure that you can stick to the processes and objectives.

Public Relations Plan

We have already discussed marketing, but it will be public relations that will keep your company's name afloat without costing you so much money. All the media are important, but establish business relationships with communication companies, reporters, and bloggers who can benefit your product through personalized recommendations since they are influential. [57]

Despite the fact that, currently, everything is managed in the networks, it does not mean that it is the only tool in which you should work. Yes, networks are a *very* important part of the development of each company and will undoubtedly provide perfect tools for the marketing plan, but focus your public relations on face-to-face events so that your clients can feel close to your brand. You may not have the budget to organize an entire event, and it may be very expensive to hire an agency to keep your advertising fresh, but today there are no excuses to forgive a brand that is lost from the public eye. You can use the following promotional means.

Sponsorship

Sponsoring events will reduce production costs, and it will maintain the image of your brand in front of potential clients. If you want to earn extra points, sponsor social responsibility events that fit the personality of your company.

Bloggers

There are people whose job is to keep the public entertained or informed through the networks. Contact those who reach your target audience and establish business relationships. They are mostly much cheaper than a radio spot or TV spot.

Coupons, Prizes, and Exclusive Discounts

These will attract your customers and, of course, consumers of similar products.

Budget

The most difficult part of the marketing plan is to make all your expectations, ideas, and projects come true. You should start by asking yourself how much each of the tools you plan to apply could come out, calculating the time it will take to do all the work, and the number of employees it will require to execute it perfectly. I don't mean spending your entire business budget on the marketing plan, but the only way to ensure that it is successful is that it has the means to meet each objective with the required precision.

Cost Cutting

Money does not grow on trees, and we cannot pretend that, as a start-up, you throw the house out the window at the first movement in the market. Thus, you require a launch in style, avoiding cravings.

Be Realistic

You cannot expect everything to be a bargain, much less depending on a capital that you do not have. So considering realistic strategies according to the current situation of the company will be the key to the good execution of the marketing plan. It may sound more complicated than it seems. As long as you keep your feet on the ground and have strong confidence in your project, others will take you as a great entrepreneur. Believing in yourself is the first strategy to get others to believe in your company and therefore in your product or service.

Loyalty Programs

As your business grows, another challenge is to retain your consumers. So one of the objectives is to get repeat customers who can identify with your brand. There are various ways to ensure that the trend continues, thanks to loyalty programs. Loyalty programs are designed to generate long-term profits, so you must be patient and, above all, persevere to see the results.

Market research reveals that it is cheaper to keep a customer than to get a new one. Therefore, focus on treating well those you already have so that they are your best advertisement. Thanks to their comments, more public can reach your entrepreneurial idea.

The main idea of loyalty programs is to increase the need to buy your products; in return, they will receive a benefit that someone else does not have. To know what you should give, you can do a market research and meet those needs. [58]

Economic Benefit

They are those in which customers benefit from special discounts and prizes or receive a free product. For example, if your business is medicine, one way to build customer loyalty is that on their fifth visit per month, they do not have to pay for one or more medicine. This is the most popular method among entrepreneurs or small businesses since it does not represent an expense, but it does little to collect additional information about your clients such as their email or birthday.

Social Benefit

It refers to those things where you give your clients invitations to events in which your business is associated. They can be tickets to a sporting event, like a major soccer game, or you can organize a cocktail or dinner only for your best clients. Through a market study, you can segment your audience and see what they like the most to do to organize an activity.

Performance

It has to do with preferential attention when visiting your business to facilitate the daily life of your clients. Airlines use them to check their passengers without having to wait long. In the case of a furniture start-up idea, the shipment can be immediate or streamline procedures to enjoy the use of your product.

Scales to Consider

When you create a loyalty program, have different scales according to the consumption made by your customers. The more they buy, the better their rewards should be.

One great advantage of market research is that it allows you to create a better loyalty program, in addition to seeking alliances with other brands or businesses that are derived from yours to deliver prizes. For instance, if you have a business that specializes in diet products, you can make an alliance with a gym so that your clients have special discounts upon registration or in the monthly payment fee. Loyalty programs have endless benefits; what you should be clear about is the time you need to apply them.

Just follow these steps when you create and present a business plan to your team, investors, stakeholders, suppliers, or clients to quickly put them in context.

CHAPTER 5

Operational Logistic and Health-Care Supply Chain Management

Eighty-five percent of the reasons for failure are deficiencies in the systems and process rather than the employee. The role of management is to change the process rather than badgering individuals to do better.

—W. Edwards Deming

Health-Care Supply Chain Management Process

At times, clients complain because you are late in product deliveries. Remember that delivering your products on time must be one of your top commitments with your clients, whether you are in the business-to-business (B2B) or business-to-consumer (B2C) market. If you face issues in this regard, it must be resolved immediately. You need to look into if there is a lack of control between production times and your product's final delivery. If things are not good in this regard, there may be a problem within your company's supply chain.

Supply chain management in health care is even more important because late deliveries can cause life-threatening conditions for patients. Therefore, in this section, we will explore the steps you must follow to achieve efficient supply chain management and add value to your health-care business. The main objective of the supply chain management is to ensure the correct functioning of logistics in a company and promote control and teamwork of all personnel responsible for this area.

In 1909, Frederick Taylor defined a company's management as an act of planning, organizing, directing, coordinating, and controlling. [59] Though many experts today consider this theory outdated, these principles regarding the plan, organization, coordination, and control have validity. A company's supply chain assumes all the management principles upheld by Taylor. This chain should work flawlessly since your customers' and suppliers' satisfaction depends on it. Let's explore the steps you need to take in your health-care business to strengthen your business processes and become a flourishing company.

First things first; the supply chain is the sum of all the activities, steps, and processes that must be carried out so that the products or services produced and distributed by a company are carried out with excellence in terms of quality, time, and place required by the final consumer.

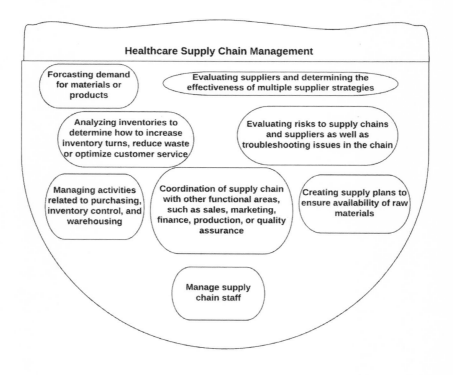

Figure 5.1: Health-Care Supply Chain Management

Supply chain management (SCM) is a process that is responsible for managing the storage and flow of all goods or services required by customers, guaranteeing the efficiency of the processes from their point of origin to the point of consumption, which requires the use of techniques that allow excellence in the integration between the different stages that occur within a supply chain like transportation, inventory, and cost. The result of applying the correct administration of the supply chain is the increase in the quality of the service or product that the company sells, providing a competitive advantage in the market. [60]

Supply chain management is usually based on three stages: supply, manufacturing, and distribution.

- **Supply:** It is based on how, when, and where the goods that serve as raw material for the manufacture of a certain product are obtained.
- **Manufacturing:** It is based on converting all that raw material into finished products that will be useful for a certain audience.
- **Distribution:** This process ensures that these products reach the hands of consumers through a variety of dealers or retail or business networks.

Supply chain management consists in the coordination and integration of many processes either within the same company or between the different companies that carry out some commercial exchange. It can be divided into three flows:

- **Product Flow:** This flow encompasses everything related to the activity of the merchandise, covering the movement of products with suppliers and customers, returns that can be made, and the needs of services.
- **Information Flow:** It is linked to all the orders' communication processes and the information that is handled with respect to the deliveries made.
- **Financial Flow:** It covers the payment schedules of the company.

All companies or organizations and people involved in the production, handling, storage, distribution, and marketing of products or services are included in the process of supply chain management; that is to say, suppliers, manufacturers, distributors, retailers, and customers. The proper design of the supply chain depends both on the needs of the customer and the roles played by those involved in each stage of the process. To create and improve the design of a supply chain, you must take into account the planning and operation of the entire company.

When you plan your supply chain management, you must consider four fundamental requirements: quantity, quality, time, and costs.

Quantity

In the case of products, you will have to have enough raw material to produce what you require and the necessary quantity of products to supply the demand of your customers. If we talk about service companies, it is about having the services necessary to satisfy your consumers' needs. If you fail in quantities, you are giving the consumer the opportunity to know the competition, and you may lose their loyalty too.

Quality

We popularly say that a product has quality when we judge that it is much better than most. In the case of a company, quality refers to standards for evaluating the proper development of the product, right from inventory procurement to delivery, with the aim of ensuring maximum customer satisfaction.

Time

You must be punctual when it comes to delivering your products. You should not get ahead because you could be saturating the clients, but you should not be late because you would be running out of supply. In the case of services, it is also crucial because the client expects an optimal and timely service.

Costs

You need to have proper control of the prices of your supplies. This activity is especially complex for companies that work with raw materials as it can compromise your product's price in the medium term.

Remember that the key to the design and operation of your supply chain is to minimize risks. Therefore, you need to evaluate each of the relationships that must occur to move on to the next step in your supply chain management process. You have different types of impacts (i.e., on revenue, on operations, on delivery, on production, on innovation, on time, on your staff, and on reputation with customers).

The major benefits of managing a supply chain include reducing costs that occur in the supply chain, fully meeting the needs of customers, and ensuring quality assurance. Supply chain management helps all processes from the acquisition of raw material to the delivery of the product to the final consumer, to be carried out in the most agile and efficient way possible. It promotes customer loyalty. As there are highly efficient production processes, it is possible to give almost immediate response times to the customer, improving delivery times. As a result, customers will always have your company in mind when they need to purchase a certain product.

Moreover, you have more effective control since the entire process is well defined. You can precisely know in real time at which point in the production chain the product is located. This guarantees greater control with suppliers, reaching a greater number of offers and monitoring the dates of entry of supplies, production, and other processes. Therefore, small daily problems are significantly reduced.

Also, it promotes teamwork. By being clear about each member of the chain's functions, you begin to work in an organized and synchronized way, ensuring that the product reaches the end consumers in the best possible conditions.

Supply chain management begins with attracting, conquering, and retaining as many customers as possible, and this happens by gathering information about the company's supply chain sector. Thus, you have to look at customers to know what product they want, how they want it, and when they want it to adjust to your supply chain measures. Having analyzed these points, you need to put everything into practice and speak with the necessary suppliers so that the desired raw materials are obtained to manage production, distribution, transport, and delivery to the consumer.

To implement an effective system, you must know this subject in depth to identify the needs that may arise in the management of the supply chain; thus, you can optimize the processes. The aspects that must be verified fundamentally are as follows:

- The quality of the suppliers
- The product manufacturing process
- The amount of inventory in stock; "not too much, not too little"
- The storage process
- The customer purchase process
- The distribution and delivery of products to the customer

Since we are in the digital revolution, supply chain management currently relies heavily on technology (i.e., the implementation of a simple barcode system greatly streamlines the process of inventory and sale of merchandise); also, the software helps in controlling the entire production and delivery process.

All companies have one or more supply chains whose performance depends on their success in this competitive world. However, not many companies give a strategic value to the way they are integrated and do not recognize how they synchronize their operations with each other to keep the end consumer satisfied without generating high costs and transferring them to their partners in the chain.

The management of the supply chain depends on several factors. The most important ones are the complexity of the product, the number of suppliers and customers, and the availability of materials. Also, there are several dimensions to consider, including the chain's complexity and length. Each company manages several chains with different characteristics about the previous points, making it more complex to define the relationships between the different entities.

Defining the relationships at each point in the chains may be different in each case and is the key to defining each type. To clearly understand the type of relationship and how to define it properly, we must have explicit knowledge of the following:

1. Members of the chain
2. The structure of the chain
3. Processes and flows of product, information, money, and decisions

Members of the Chain

It includes all the members that, in one way or another, interact directly or indirectly from the point of origin to the point of consumption.

A fairly complex network can be formed; however, they can be classified into two groups:

1. Primary are those who add value directly to the product or service.
2. Secondary are those who provide resources, knowledge, or assets to the chain's primary members such as banks, logistic operators, IT outsourcing companies, and so on.

In some cases, a company may be a primary participant in one process and a secondary or support participant in another. The distinction between primary and support is not obvious in all cases; however, it must provide important criteria to define the relationship and the role they must play in each process.

The Structure of the Chain

There are two essential dimensions to describe, understand, analyze, and manage the supply chain, that is, the horizontal and the vertical.

- Horizontal refers to the number of tiers through the entire chain of a product.
- The vertical structure refers to the number of suppliers and customers involved in each tier. A company may have a product group with a narrow vertical structure with few companies on each tier and other products with many customers and suppliers on each tier.

The structure of the chains is one of the factors that determine the complexity of the chain.

Processes and Flows

Supply chains are dynamic and immersed in a continuous flow of materials, information, money, and decisions. Each organization executes different processes to interact with other organizations. Success requires a drastic change in the way we currently work based on functions within an organization to become an intercompany team, integrating activities in key processes that add value and that can be measured in speed, cost, and service.

Any chain's success depends on redesigning processes to improve productivity, control costs, and reduce execution times. The processes must be analyzed and designed by looking not only at how to integrate their activities to add value but also more importantly how it is effectively related to the previous process and to the following process in such a way that it contributes to the improvement of the cost and service relationship of the entire chain. The vast majority of inefficiencies in supply chains are generated by the links or relationships between the different processes, especially those that have to do with more than one organization. Thus, designing these interrelationships well is key to the success of the supply chain integration strategy. Making a design with a holistic approach is key, and this suggests taking into account at the same time the flows that appear immersed in the chains (i.e., materials, information, money, and decisions).

Process reengineering focusing on supply chain management is essential in companies that want to continue in the market. For this, they must understand very well the ever-changing conditions of the global market and design their strategy following the cycle mentioned below:

- Evaluate your supply chains
- Plan the redesign of your processes and flows
- Operate the new design
- Measure and improve

Although companies, in one way or another, have managed relationships with their business partners for years, they have not formalized a series of basic criteria to ensure that the optimum is gained through the chain. Thus, you can use the aforementioned four-point criteria to direct your business toward designing competitive supply chains.

Building a Competitive Supply Chain Infrastructure

Infrastructure means business processes that are defined as demand management, deliveries, manufacturing, supply, returns, accounts payable, and accounts receivable. You can make these processes competitive by focusing on your client. All customers interact in a supply chain as they order a product, receive it, return it if it is defective, and pay for it. Therefore, a process map that defines each type of interaction in the cycle is a good tool to define infrastructure. A company makes its infrastructure more competitive when it simplifies its processes, reduces the number of interventions in the processes, and increases the speed of the information transmitted between them, and that is basic for planning.

Designing Relationships of Logistics Network

To streamline logistics, you must know where demand and supply are geographically located. You design your supply chain by connecting all supply sources to all destinations of demand and all the business partners that intervene between them. Once the entire network is understood, you can analyze volumes to determine strategic routes and modes of transportation. The supply chain works to optimize costs vs. times, developing and managing relationships with a preferred and the reduced number of distributors and transporters. This design can provide an important competitive advantage for lowering freight costs, import and export taxes, and storage and can mean significant savings. By reducing the total number of links or nodes in the chain, you can save logistics costs by consolidating cargo volumes and reducing the total number of routes. By capturing accurate and high-speed information at the point of sale, the need to store products throughout the chain can be replaced.

Synchronization of Supply with Demand

A good supply chain must match the supply rate with the demand rate at each node. Hence, you need to synchronize the product mix that is in production and the mix that the customer requests. If any link in the chain overproduces relative to market demand, inventory is accumulated. But when a link produces less than what is demanded, the coverage of the total chain is affected; in this case, one of the partners will restrict the system. The supply chain reaches its best execution in throughput (i.e., the speed at which the chain generates money through sales) if each of the partners exactly matches the throughput of the system constraint. Synchronizing the supply chain is the secret to improving customer service without increasing investment in inventory.

Production only builds and the logistics channel only moves what the company has sold. The demand of customers pushes inventories through the channel, but again, the system depends on the precision and speed of the information provided by each partner in the chain. Thus, the total supply chain—including the retailer, distributor, distribution center, and plant—must synchronize to equalize the promotion time. On the other hand, you will experience a surge in hidden supply chain costs for overtime, freight forwarding, and warehouse space, which may end in poor customer service and lost profits.

Measuring Performance Globally

A broad supply chain in a company transcends local departments, the cross-functional team, the divisional structure, the corporate business climate, and even the national culture. Yet frequently, performance measures continue to be strictly defined to optimize local operations and reward individual execution. Measurements guide behavior. In this way, for a group of business partners who make up a supply chain to synchronize and optimize, they must align and define the same execution measures. This is the Achilles' heel of supply chain management. This makes it necessary for you to generate a lot of trust among your partners and make great efforts in managing relationships across different business and national cultures.

Surely, one of the most important points that a supply chain manager has to plan with great care is the work team (i.e., the management of supply chain staff). To build an efficient work team, will and attitude are essential. I have always preferred to form a team of people essentially sustained by members with a will and a positive attitude, followed by professionalism and experience. I want to be understood in the sense that you can have the four aforementioned skills; in fact, it will be desirable, but it should always be sought, as a necessary condition, that each member of the team that you want to train has good values and will above all. It is also desirable that these values and attitudes are homogeneous among all team members to align goals.

If you manage to align personal and individual goals with those of the team, you will have the project well balanced since all the people who make it up will row toward the same destination. It will be the team leader's job to investigate and ask each member what personal goals may or may not align with the team's own goals.

Diversity is a great key to success so you can mix to unite ages and experiences. It is effective to have team members who have different professional experiences and ages. With members with different experiences, you can obtain different points of view and knowledge, which helps avoid the single thought that usually arises in teams. Also, this removes limitations and facilitates the emergence of new ideas. On the other hand, having a wide spectrum of ages within the team members facilitates different work rates and motivations according to what each task, activity, or project requires.

It will always be desirable to have a multidisciplinary team since all members will contribute something different to the team and be flexible enough. When you have diverse roles and personalities, you can have prototypes of different people. Having personalities among the team members can establish different roles that allow the smooth flow and protocols of daily work within the team.

One aspect to be observed with great care is the remuneration of each member of the team. Here, the most important thing is that members who perform similar tasks and objectives have a similar, if not equal, remuneration. And it will be necessary to estimate the responsibility of each member for the common goal. There will be responsibilities that will have to be rewarded better and others less. That is undoubted, and if not, it will be the team leader's job to explain this incentive system.

To sum up, the number of nodes or relationships that the chain defines must be minimized. The business processes that define the supply chain interactions to deliver, return, and pay should be simplified and streamlined. The backward and forward logistics network should be built around a select group and a reduced number of distributors and transporters, and when possible, the volume should be maximized through the routes.

All partners must agree to plan and control so that supply is synchronized with customer demands. All partners in the chain must understand how their execution can be the restriction of the chain and that successful execution depends on the precision and speed with which each one handles the information.

The partners must agree on global implementation measures from the client's perspective. The fortune of a company, which is only one link in the chain, depends on the synchronized execution of the other partners. I hope you will experience no mistakes and no lack of control by following these guidelines, and you will minimize the risks in your business, and your customers will feel more satisfied.

Since SCM involves all departments within the health-care business and even outside providers, you need to take everybody on board with confidence (i.e., team members and supply providers) to understand the ways to synergize and get optimal productivity out of your business. There are already many challenges to deal with in the health-care system, and you need to be ready to take risks as well. To ensure a smooth SCM process, involve related stakeholders and strategies. In this way, the solutions will be much more effective and satisfying.

CHAPTER 6

Health-Care Technology and Innovations

Adopting a continuous learning mindset is and will continue to be needed to adjust to the changing healthcare landscape. Staff will need to possess and continually refine competencies in IT in order to contribute and compete. For our patients, who will be expected to handle more self-care through IT capabilities, the need to develop comfort with wearables and using self-monitoring, AI and care management will be essential. In short, the biggest challenge facing healthcare will be in embracing the embeddedness of IT in all facets of the health care and the delivery system.

—Linda C. Lombardi

It is true that technology is the center of new businesses. As the businesses are quickly growing and big brands are entering the market, it seems a bit difficult to enter the market. However, technology and science are always on the rise, and there will always be room for new players to claim their fair share of the market. From sophisticated device portfolios to telemedicine solutions, many companies are working on solutions to turn the sector around. From all angles, health is a sector that is very much ready to have a roll in the hands of technology. Thus, there are many emerging technologies—such as electronic health record, electronic medical record (EMR), artificial intelligence (AI), wearables, big data, virtual reality, and 3D printing—that are being introduced in the health-care sector by established brands and entrepreneurs. [61]

Today science and technology go hand in hand, so why not invest your time and money in this area? Indeed, for health-care entrepreneurs, business ideas based on technology still have great room. Thus, it is time to focus on medical technology, growing in multiple ways, from surgical devices and diagnostic machines to sales of supplies and patient data analysis programs. Let me tell you that opportunities in medicine and technology are endless.

Thus, many big firms have been creating specialized solutions for several years pertaining to devices and processes to take the health-care sector to its technological transformation. But you must choose your specialization with due diligence. There are many ways to create businesses in technology and medicine, but you must avoid getting carried away by ambition. To be successful in technological medicine, you must focus on something very specific. If you are good at sales, for example, find a way to expand the use of technology in medical sales; maybe it could be with diagnostic equipment or specialized programs to sell medical supplements. In any case, medicine is a large and competitive sector, so being focused on something specialized will make your idea more practical.

Before getting fully involved in medical technology, you should look at the data and trends. In this case, it is worth investing in those diseases or conditions that are most prevalent in society, those that are beginning to be discovered, and those that are sought to eradicate with more dedication and budget. So keeping an eye on the data and numbers can help you make better decisions.

As in any business, it is essential to know how and when to make the first move. If you think of investing in something like technology in medicine, seek the opinion of an expert. As tech-savvy as you may be, science goes hand in hand, so make sure you know which direction to go and be careful not to pursue something that will not grow or is very complicated. Thus, you talk to doctors, admins, and managers in hospitals, pharmacists, and head nurses as these people deal with issues in medical affairs every day. They surely know better than anyone what is needed and if your idea makes sense.

Technology in health care has led to incredible advancement, and big brands are already exploiting the available opportunities. Let me show you a few big brands to help you see the potential.

Johnson & Johnson

Johnson & Johnson is the largest company in the medical device industry. They have a medical devices section, namely, global medical solutions, global orthopedics, and global surgery. Its subsidiaries include Biosense Webster, a leader in the production of advanced cardiac diagnostic, therapy, and mapping tools.

GE Healthcare

Some products from this company include Discovery IGS 740 (a mobile angiography system), dual-probe Vscan (the world's first portable ultrasound machine with two transducers in one probe), and Invenia ABUS (an ultrasound machine).

Medtronic

Medtronic is a large global medical device company with executive offices in Ireland and operational headquarters in Minneapolis. With more than 100,000 employees in more than 160 countries, Medtronic's cardiac and vascular division stands out with implantable devices such as Amplia MRI and Compia MRI Quad CRT-D, and Micra transcatheter pacing system (TPS) pacemakers.

Siemens

Siemens, a Germany-based company founded in 1847, is the largest European medical device company with 293,000 employees around the world. A great part of its success is attributed to its diagnostic imaging business.

Philips Healthcare

Philips Healthcare is a large company, spread over one hundred countries. Philips has produced more than 450 products and services. [62]

Here, you can see that the most advanced medical technology firms are able to grow exponentially in profit and size. In this context, getting started may seem a bit difficult while obstacles are sometimes scary and problems overwhelm, but you must not let yourself be slowed down; instead, adopt the true mindset of becoming an entrepreneur in the health-care sector. Let's see what options you can consider for your entrepreneurial venture in the use of technology in medicine.

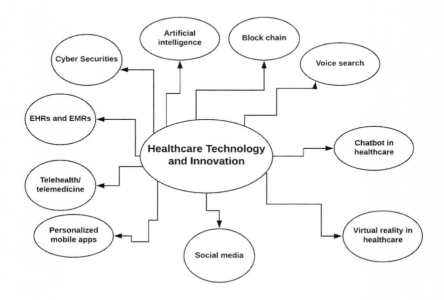

Figure 6.1

Health-Care Technology and Innovation

As technology is involved in almost every business and consumers use it to find and contact businesses and services, health care has also benefited from technology. In fact, technology-driven entrepreneurs have the best chances to enter the field with their innovative ideas. For example, we have seen that EHRs have gained good ground already, whereas the real potential is much more than simple software. Let's see the areas you can consider to start your technology-based health-care venture.

Artificial Intelligence

The Industrial Revolution was conceived as a threat by workers at that time when machines were introduced in factories. Today the Industrial Revolution has been fully integrated into our world. Similarly, once conceived as a futuristic threat to humanity, AI has now become a part of our daily life. In the health-care sector, AI is helping change the practices with its useful applications. AI helps medical practitioners make informed decisions and improve accuracy.

With the continuous integration of AI into health care, it is now smarter and not more difficult to care for patients. In fact, the use of AI in health care and patient-specific products derived from 3D printing or the consolidation of robotic surgery is some of the innovations that will improve healing and change health care further.

Thus, AI is already present in many areas of health care, not something of the future. There are AI devices for patients with personal wellness systems and devices for doctors and specialists in medical diagnosis and treatment systems. Before doing anything with AI-based products, tons of data and patient information are stored and classified in isolation in different systems.

We are already witnessing innovations in medicine powered by AI. Among them, Lenovo, in collaboration with TechsoMed, has designed a revolutionized tumor removal process, thanks in part to supercomputers and sensors, which have revolutionized diagnostics. [63] It is a result of AI programs that the systems execute to comb data with high efficiency to detect changes and label them for careful review.

The health-care technology company Digital Surgery in London, UK, also developed and successfully demonstrated the dynamic, real-time AI system designed for operating rooms. The AI platform can provide route maps and act as a navigation system for each operating room and surgical center. Additionally, it addresses the myriad variables that surgical teams face, from staff turnover, language, culture, tools, and resources to the level of training and skills of the professional medical team. [64]

On the patient side, we can see an explosion of data (i.e., everything from mobile phones to watches to weighing scales) now integrated with sensors and the internet connectivity that allow consumers to create a detailed and personalized health data network. Information such as weight, heart rate, activity level, and even much more sophisticated data is stored there.

AI is currently on the rise so much so that even the world's largest medical research networks are powered by AI. The Owkin Loop network platform enables experts from leading hospitals and research institutions in the United States and Europe to train predictive models on real-world data and transfer accumulated knowledge to collective intelligence. [65] Thus, in the health-care sector, AI is here to stay, and it is just the beginning.

Block Chain

We hear a lot about the block chain as the cryptocurrency and transaction registration system, and it is gaining new horizons in the health-care sector as well. The application of block chain has extended to many areas of our daily lives, and its future is booming. Medical facilities are using it as a way to guarantee data security among doctors and patients, medical staff, and health plans since health data is monitored from numerous sources like wearables, genetic tests, wellness apps, and the list can go on and on.

The idea of using block chain is that the platforms house a kind of unique digital medical record. Thus, the patient would have all his history of medical examinations, illnesses, and other information about his health in one place. Other technologies can allow this type of functionality, but the block chain has attracted the most interest from the medical community.

The British company Medicalchain operates with the concept "own your health." Medicalchain offers patients the technology to store their medical history and make it available the way they prefer. [66] Slovenian Iryo also offers this technology with the aim of ensuring access to information from anywhere in the world. [67]

Chatbots

In many health-care services, chatbots are used to reserve appointments or administrative inquiries, but COVID-19 has accelerated the application of chatbots, given the need to optimize medical and care resources. Thus, many health providers have implemented chatbots to meet the high demand for consultations that the pandemic is generating.

Chatbots can function as a means of official information. The search for information to appease uncertainty has become widespread during the health emergency. Official bodies and health providers are receiving many inquiries that, in general, are repeated. Thus, implementing chatbots is a very efficient way to entertain those queries, giving clear, precise, and official information. [68] In this way, resources are optimized with the transmission of reliable information, and the users get an immediate response at any time of the day.

A chatbot can and will never replace medical care, but it serves the useful role of being the first line of medical care without human contact. In a situation where attempts are made to prevent the risk of contagion and health personnel must focus on priority cases, it is useful that the first line of care can be solved through self-service.

Since the advent of COVID-19, chatbots are also useful in entertaining symptomatological queries; through relevant and intelligently formulated questions, they allow to rule out cases that do not require immediate attention and determine which ones do need to be treated with priority. The implementation of chatbots in digital channels for the first line of medical attention frees up the telephone lines for cases that require more in-depth attention. Thus, through chatbots, the simplest queries are solved by other digital channels. The human-assisted telephone is reserved for dealing with more delicate inquiries.

By centralizing the information of potential patients through chatbots, essential data is automatically collected for further evaluation and monitoring. Chatbots help better manage the flow of inquiries for human resources, which if not handled efficiently can cause an organization's system to collapse.

Where solutions must be fast, interactive text response (ITR) chatbots that interact through options without implementing natural language understanding (NLU) chatbots are the most functional. [69] Since they don't involve the development of AI, they don't require a training process, and interaction can be controlled and limited based on the specific objectives for which it was created.

For a reliable chatbot diagnosis, it is key to ask the patient the right questions about what they are feeling and their possible exposure to contagion. The questionnaire must be prepared by health professionals according to official procedures.

Virtual Reality (VR)

Virtual reality is a representation of scenes and images of objects and environments produced by a computer system that gives the simulation of real existence. VR consists in sensory immersion, generated artificially from real or nonreal environments, which we can access by means of various technological devices and become part of it. Generally speaking, VR is considered to be a technology for entertainment. However, in addition to the application for video games, tourism sector, and so on, VR has gained its ground in the health-care world with multiple uses.

As for the patient experience, through the use of VR, the test to be performed can be shown, facilitating greater relaxation by having more information; likewise, it allows greater involvement of the patient in decision-making.

VR's immersive capacity through different technological devices can involve all senses, which helps medical experts in the treatment of psychological disorders, post-traumatic stress disorder, and phobias. For example, the aforementioned immersive capacity offers the possibility of direct exposure therapies to different situations in a safe way for both patients and professionals.

Above all, VR is an interesting learning tool as it provides an experience very close to the real one. This technology allows us to experience different physical or sensory reactions, in addition to having automatic learning algorithms. Thus, it opens up endless possibilities for health-care professionals (i.e., they can review and practice surgeries before the actual process, which allows greater safety and a reduction in their time for training of the complex skills, such as laparoscopies or endoscopies without the need of real patients).

The capacity of VR can even make it possible to perform surgeries or other interventions at a distance. Its recreation of real situations can allow the professional to attend a more or less complex operation without having to travel to the place on-site. It is not hard to imagine the implications that something like this would have on global health-care systems. Many other VR uses are possible (i.e., in physiotherapy and rehabilitation of cardiovascular accidents, in therapies to overcome addictions, in meditation to calm pain and anxiety, among others). [70]

Social Media Networks

Social media networks and health care have established a strong relationship in recent years, and undoubtedly, they are affecting the way we manage our health. In the sector of health care, patients can experience three main uses of social media networks (i.e., consultation, information, and support). Today more and more health professionals have created their pages on social media for consultation on networks such as Facebook and Twitter. These platforms provide the possibility for medical professionals to put their knowledge and their spare time at the service of their followers to solve their problems. Similarly, people follow social media pages to seek information on many health topics such as weight loss and diabetes control, among others.

Another use of social media networks is the creation of groups of people based on common interests and particular themes. This feature has been used by many patients to create support groups on networks like Facebook, where they can talk with other people in the same situation and share material of interest.

If a hazard of social media is to be highlighted, it is the possibility of publishing excess and unauthentic info since nobody controls what is said on social networks. Thus, this loophole can cause the spread of all kinds of inaccurate, erroneous information. It is especially serious when it comes to health information like health tips. It means that the pairing of social media networks and health care is still viewed with misgivings by the medical community.

Medical experts have been seen as somewhat reluctant to use new information technologies, and this is another possible reason for them to avoid their presence on social media. However, the participation of medical experts is necessary if the internet is to truly become an important public health-care tool. Thus, health-care entrepreneurs have great room for creating exclusive social media platforms for health-care professionals and patients.

Telemedicine

The studies by the WHO show that the good intellectual formation of communities is linked, in a direct and unfailing way, to good health and nutrition. If the working population is not in good health, it will never have sustainable and growing progress over time. Poor health refers, in an integral way, to poor nutrition and the suffering of disabling, treatable, and preventable diseases in adults and children.

Thus, governments enact policies to improve health coverage and the quality of medical care; but factors like high population dispersion, distances, and shortage of specialists in all areas of medicine run counter to these political wills. As health problems grow, governments channel economic resources and enact laws that seek to alleviate the sector's difficulties in terms of coverage in the short and long term and try to launch quality medical care to which all human citizens are entitled, regardless of their economic status and geographical location. For this reason, telemedicine plays a fundamental role in what concerns the sustainable improvement of the health of communities globally. Telemedicine is a great tool for the good scientific performance of health-care personnel to solve existing issues in the health-care sector since telemedicine allows patients to receive health care from a distance, without the need to be in person in a clinic.

Telemedicine is any medical act performed without direct physical contact between the professional and the patient, or between professionals among themselves, through some telematic system. The concept of telemedicine has been implemented to play a fundamental role in the sustainable improvement of health care for communities, especially rural communities. To offer telemedicine, medical professionals employ information and communications technology for the exchange of valid information for the diagnosis, treatment, prevention, evaluation, and education of public health-care providers. Thus, pertaining to technology, telemedicine is a vast ground for health-care entrepreneurs to find great opportunities.

CHAPTER 7

Medical Informatics, Data Science, Decision-Making, and Quality Improvement

Health informatics is about bringing data and new technologies to efforts to improve human health.

—Kishor Vaidya

Data science is a wide-ranging discipline that interconnects with several other fields, and health care is no exception. Among many methods of data science, according to OHSU.edu, a unanimous one is

> the multi-disciplinary field that uses scientific methods, processes, algorithms, and systems to extract knowledge and insights from data in various forms, both structured and unstructured. [71]

Thus, data science is an effective tool for medical informatics, decision-making, and quality improvement in the health-care sector. Today as an entrepreneur, you must understand the great potential of using data in any field.

There are various forms of using data and information that you can use to find your ground in health-care entrepreneurship, such as the following:

- *Health informatics* is an umbrella term referring to informatics practice across the health-care landscape.
- Medical informatics is practiced by doctors.
- Clinical informatics is practiced within a health-care organization, typically by clinicians.
- Nursing informatics is practiced by nurses who employ tools and systems of informatics.
- Public health informatics, also known as population health informatics, is employed for improving the health of the public.
- Biomedical informatics is about applying the practice to life sciences. [72]

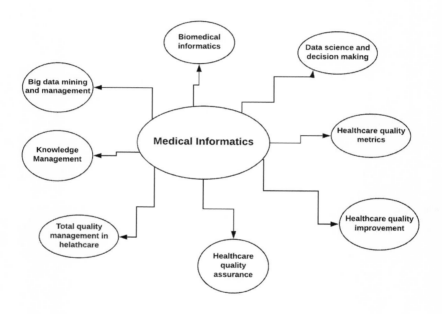

Figure 7.1

Medical Informatics

The field of medical informatics has been revolutionizing the medicine world at a fast speed, creating new insights to improve health-care quality and cost. Thus, medical informatics also helps in discovering causes and cures of various diseases as well as new opportunities for professionals and business opportunities for health-care entrepreneurs. To be precise and simple, medical informatics is about the profound implications of applying informatics to the medicine world; however, you may come across a variety of its definition. In fact, the American Medical Informatics Association (AMIA) has a different thing to say about it:

> The informatics community typically uses the term health informatics to refer to applied research and practice of informatics across the clinical and public health domains. Medical informatics is an earlier term, no longer routinely used, outdated by the growth of bioinformatics. [73]

Medical informatics is found at the intersection of health care and technology. In medical informatics, medical and computer sciences collaborate to improve health care and patient outcomes, which makes it a hybrid field. Thus, it uses technology to its best capacity for patient care in clinical and research settings. The professionals in medical informatics have the following responsibilities:

- Create, facilitate, and maintain the best ways for medical facilities to keep her
- Improve communication between health-care service providers and facilities for the best patient outcomes
- Store, manage, and analyze data for conducting well-directed research
- Help in intricate and technology-dependent research

Biomedical Informatics (BMI)

Data science is a tad different from biomedical informatics (BMI). According to OHSU.edu, BMI is

> the interdisciplinary field that studies and pursues the effective uses of biomedical data, information, and knowledge for scientific inquiry, problem-solving and decision making, motivated by efforts to improve human health. [74]

It is evident that these disciplines overlap and complement each other as well. BMI deals with a wider range of data and information tasks that are focused on the things learned from data and how they are applied in a wider socio-technical context.

Though BMI has been there for decades, it is still a progressive field. The American Health Information Management Association (AHIMA) was founded in 1928 as the American Association of Medical Record Librarians, which dealt with paper-based medical records. Today we have the electronic medical record that has broadened the overall scope of the field.

In September 1961, Kaiser Permanente found a department of medical method research whose goal was to start the usage of computers in the practice of medicine. In 1962, they received their first federal grants for automating and improving screening methods. [75]

From analog computers to today's digital revolution and EHR systems, BMI has come a long way, and you can take it a step further with your entrepreneurial ideas.

Big Data Mining

In the field of medicine, a massive amount of data is produced that involves information of patients' history, ongoing treatment, and a lot more; obviously, it needs to be stored since it contains valuable information. When this data is properly categorized, it helps in understanding medical concerns, leading to substantial success in the restorative field, mainly in the areas of illness analysis and aversion. Thus, big data science is a crucial and highly progressive area for health care as well as health-care entrepreneurs. Through technology, we can examine the enormous medical data faster and infer it for the well-being of people.

Data mining is a method of extracting targeted data from a big data set. [76] In big data mining, we traverse the big volume of data through methods of association, classification, clustering, sequential patterns, and decision trees.

- Association: In this method, correlation is made between data items and their patterns.
- Classification: It is used as a feeder or an outcome of other methods like the decision tree.

- Clustering: It is used for recognizing a group of associated results, and it is also valuable to recognize distinctive data.
- Sequential Patterns: They help in identifying trends and are used on longer-term data.
- Decision trees: They are used as a part of the determination criteria as they help in utilizing the choice of particular information inside a general structure. [77]

Knowledge Management

In the health-care sector, finding the right solutions and making the best decisions is seriously dependent on access to relevant knowledge at the right time. In today's time, it is essential for the health-care sector to manage internally and externally generated knowledge so as to provide the best health-care services with operational excellence. Like big data mining, knowledge management is here to play a crucial role. In 1991, the field of knowledge management was established as a proper discipline.

As the name implies, knowledge management refers to a process of capturing, developing, sharing, and using knowledge as and when needed. Its core purposes include improved performance, innovation, and competitive advantage. As we have seen since the beginning of this chapter, the usage of data is an extremely important part of innovative ideas, and knowledge management is all about managing data. Thus, there is a lot of room for health-care entrepreneurs to find success on these grounds.

Knowledge management is helpful in the decision-making process. When there is information overload or lack of knowledge, it can cause serious issues for medical health-care professionals to make an informed decision. On the other hand, when they are supported by access to relevant knowledge and data, they will be able to make more informed decisions. [78]

Total Quality Management in Health Care

We know that a health-care system is of fundamental interest to all medical facilities and society, meaning that the masses are involved in it. Thus, ensuring total quality management (TQM) in a health-care system is not an option. Be it private or public sector, a hospital management system must ensure the presence of TQM at every step and level. To meet this need, medical facilities, as well as other health-care-related organizations, have been increasingly implementing TQM. The best part is that a properly implemented TQM also helps in reducing costs, improving proficiency, and providing the best quality of patient care.

With the advent of digital systems, TQM has gained strong ground, but it is not a new concept in the health-care sector. Its roots date as far back as the time of Florence Nightingale's work in the Crimean War (1854–56). Since the health-care sector is gigantic, there is great room for health-care entrepreneurs to move in this direction.

An effective system for TQM is a vital part of a medical facility since TQM offers it a competitive and strategic advantage over others. For health-care entrepreneurs, it means a great market share with a high margin of profitability. [79]

Health-Care Quality Assurance

Today we rank almost everything per their outcomes, and we do the same for medical services we receive. In fact, the process of ranking has become even faster with the use of the internet. As far as the medical facilities are concerned, they are ranked per their outcomes for patients. Thus, patients can easily select the best options for themselves according to their needs and resources. In this context, no medical facilities and related services can afford to leave loose ends pertaining to quality assurance. Thus, quality assurance is an essential part of the health-care sector so that every person involved can ensure the best health-care services to the patients and improve further.

A QA team or program works through the whole health-care system to design policies and processes that can lead to the best outcomes for patients. Quality assurance signifies compliance with a host of regulations, policies, and laws at various levels that may include the federal, state, and local. Also, it helps develop internal strategies to support high-quality health-care services. For health-care entrepreneurs, creating a quality assurance program or service is an open business invitation.

Health-Care Quality Improvement

As for the next step of health-care quality assurance, we can see health-care quality improvement (QI). According to AHRQ.gov, to this effect, in health care:

QI is the framework to systematically improve the ways care is delivered to patients. Processes have characteristics that can be measured, analyzed, improved, and controlled. QI entails continuous efforts to achieve stable and predictable process results to reduce process variation and improve the outcomes of these processes for patients and the healthcare organization and system.

Medical science is indeed a part of technological evolution, but it still does not address patients' requirements, safety, overall system efficiency, and desired improvement in quality over time. Thus, today entrepreneurs can find a huge gap in health-care QI; in fact, the QI in health care needs overhauling or redesigning. Though EMR and EHR are already there and playing a great role in the system's development, we can still go the extra mile.

QI helps in accelerating the overall performance as it advances with a systematic approach and careful monitoring and assessment and offers solutions for further improvement. Its work is cyclic that is aimed at seeking a higher level of performance through every cycle. [80]

You, as an entrepreneur today, can support the health-care sector through digital and technological advancements. In this chapter, you can, I hope, see the importance of using data to your advantage and create an innovative solution to enter the health-care sector. As responsible citizens and entrepreneurs, let's come up with ideas that can improve the health-care system, even if not in its entirety.

CHAPTER 8

Practice Management

Health-care organizations deploy practice management to organize registration, scheduling, patient tracking, accounting of patients, and reporting with the help of a single workflow across all operations. This enables a single platform to collect payments on all patient accounts. Thus, practice management essentially refers to management of all the business aspects of the medical practice.

Simply put, practice management encompasses every aspect of running a clinic outside of medical delivery. Practically, you will see people in the roles below handling practice management tasks:

- Practice manager
- Administrator
- Chief operating officer
- Executive director

As practice management can significantly boost your health-care service revenue, it is important to understand how every specific function may help you become more well organized and profitable, along with the improvement regarding patient care.

Finance

Suppose you are schooled in medical sciences; however, when you see a balance sheet, it may look like a mixture of incoherent tables, numbers, or percentages. It can be said that the financials of the business may not be where your strength is. It also doesn't help that the medical industry has more complicated payment processes. Practice management systems can also help facilitate organizing your medical facility's finances. The best health-care practice management will help in speeding the process up and remove inefficiencies, saving time and money in the longer run.

Compliance

There is an extra layer of compliance requirement that varies by province or state and country due to the sensitive nature of records of health care. Personal health information may include the following:

- Family history
- Personal identification information
- Service plan
- Payment information
- Health-care eligibility
- Information about body parts or substances
- Health numbers

Information Technology

IT continues to increase in importance each day as we develop and adopt new tech-based solutions that help organize medical facilities. They can help with the following:

- Scheduling appointment and taking in assessments
- Quickly assessing insurance eligibility
- Processing electronic claims
- Organizing and protecting electronic health records
- Cost-effective practices as you scale

Marketing

Marketing help spread awareness, attract customers, and build the brand. All this is in the service of enhancing your medical facility's profitability. Marketing has increased in complexity. Moreover, it pays to have a marketing expert supporting your practice manager who has expertise in these different tactics and strategies on your side.

Operations

Business operations mean how your business produces profit (i.e., what services do you offer, and how do you extract value from said services?). By offering patient care as the service and looking for ways to reduce the costs of providing that service, you can increase your profits. Someone who works in operations will be in charge of finding cost-cutting actions without reducing the quality of service being provided.

Models for Hospitals

Hospital executives don't believe that they can succeed with value-based care until their practice management system communicates with their other systems. The physicians are accountable for value-based care for both the clinical and financial outcomes of a patient's care. Understanding a patient's health and also their expenditures is the key to success under alternative payment models. Hospitals realize more than value-based care benefits from integrating their practice management systems with their revenue cycle management and EHR technologies. Hospitals and health-care systems are gradually obtaining physician practices to leverage economies of scale, contribute to value-based care, and offer more services to patients—resources consumed compared with when providers operated on unconnected and disparate practice management software.

Models for Urgent Care

Pure-Play Model

The pure-play model typically entails urgent care service providers functioning as intermediaries between the emergency room and the physician's office. It allows those in need of emergency services to access care in a time. The pure-play model depends on midlevel providers to reduce costs and allows for higher operating margins. However, the model is challenged by more competition, dynamic models of urgent care, and increased state regulations.

Rural Model

Rural urgent care functions the same as the pure-play model. The only difference is that rural urgent care is located in sparsely populated areas and is commonly considered the most suitable source of timely and quality care services. Urgent care effectively works together with hospitals to ensure that access to quality and affordable health care is increased in rural areas, thus developing greater access to health care between vulnerable populations in rural areas.

Hybrid Model

Hybrid model urgent care provides for the scheduled and walk-in patients in need of health-care services. The model can be located as a storefront or a standard medical practice. The hybrid model helps the newer practices opportunity to increase market share by extending hours and accepting walk-ins. Providers that are independent may consider the model rather than integrating it with a hospital system.

Specialized Model

The specialized urgent care model operates similarly to the pure-play model, but it concentrates on providing specialized care services. Medical facilities for orthopedics or pediatrics can be examples of specialized urgent care. The model should be in a well-populated area for optimal utilization.

Moreover, this model will not have the same impact, such as access to primary care, as other urgent care models.

On-Site Model

The model concentrates on adding a clinic on-site at organizations, ensuring that quality health-care services are offered where they are needed the most. The model may reduce total health-care costs for employers and enhance employee satisfaction. The on-site model is convenient for the patients as it ensures that affordable quality health-care services are accessible, though this model limits access to those employees of the business offering this service.

Models for Outpatient

Practice managers also play a vital role in outpatient care. They are in charge of appointment scheduling, medical facility, medical record management, and financial management, among others. These functions have become more important to a value-based care model. Efficient practice managers balance appointment demand, improve medical facility's efficiency, and optimize time management for physicians with a measurable effect on patient and physician satisfaction.

Unproductive practice management can lead to poor patient satisfaction, overloaded staff, and billing errors. These types of problems reduce revenue, raise costs, frustrate physicians, and may cause patients to seek care at other places. The improvement comes from optimal practice management for the provider's productivity.

Building and Retaining Patients' Panel

Compare demand with the provider's supply of appointments for the coming year. Although patients will naturally move away or change insurance plans, reducing demand on the practice, changes may need to be made to ensure that appointment demand can be met. These might include the following:

- Closing the panel of the overpaneled provider
- Excusing the overpaneled provider from absentee coverage of other providers
- Adding new providers
- Adding new support staff to increase the efficiency of existing providers
- Exploring new ways to increase the efficiency of existing providers; the no-cost methods of increasing provider efficiency include shared charting responsibilities, keeping to schedule, managing no-shows, and discouraging walk-ins
- Adding new exam rooms
- Determining if the overpaneled situation truly is an overload situation, reviewing tolerances of the overpaneled provider, and being sure to inspect all aspects of the final panel number
- Removing patients from the overpaneled provider; the panel manager, provider, or care team design should tell the patients about the change, encourage them to choose a new provider, and support engagement with the new provider or care team
- Comparing the final panel roster total with the calculated right size; the final panel numbers may not essentially be accurate in representing that a provider is over- or underpaneled.

Before making decisions of mitigating overpaneling, consider the following steps:

- Evaluating the data by age group
- Asking the provider and care team members about the panel size in relation to their workload and ability to function as a team
- Asking the patients about their experience in the newly paneled practice

Ongoing Monitoring and Adjustment

The panel manager is in charge of ongoing monitoring, analysis, and adjustment of provider panels. It is necessary to run panel reports every month to check for outliers. After the process is entrenched, a quarterly review of panel size will be sufficient. Annually, the practice may elect to review provider supply for the coming year to ensure that there is sufficient appointment availability to meet the demands of the current panel size. The panel manager again and again monitors and makes panel adjustments.

Provider Status Changes

- FTE adjustments, terminations, leaves of absence, transfers to other locations of the medical facility
- Onboarding new providers
- Transfer of care upon request by the provider

Patient Status Changes

- New patients
- Adolescent transition to adult care
- Transfer of care upon request by patient or family
- The patient self-discontinues care by seeking health services in another practice or moving out of the area
- Demise

The panel manager will be associating with a number of unassigned patients occasionally to ensure that the organization meets its empanelment goals. The continuity trends are evaluated at the provider and practice levels, and interventions are applied as appropriate to ensure continuity.

Open/Closed Panels

The panel manager is in charge of comparing panel size and anticipated demand for each provider daily. When there is evidence that a provider panel is overloaded, the panel may be closed to new patients at the decision of the provider, the medical director, or the management team.

CHAPTER 9

Human Factors

If your employees are satisfied and they really like their job, they're going to treat their patients well, which will increase patient satisfaction and the quality of care they're providing.
—Tyler Newton

The most important functions of the HR department are to organize, evaluate, plan, structure, and satisfy everything related to the organization's personnel (i.e., staff). The HR selects and hires the staff required in each position, ensuring that each person has the profile, knowledge, and experience appropriate for their work; provide workers with the tools and means they require to carry out their work fully; satisfy the needs of the employee in various economic, professional, social, and family aspects, among others; and stimulate productivity in employees.

A company may have the best facilities, machinery, and furniture; but if you don't have a good HR department, you won't be able to progress efficiently. Why? Because they make it possible for the company to get the talented staff and manage it to go ahead.

To start with, you need to determine your staffing needs, considering the following aspects:

- How much manpower is required?
- What profile should you have?
- What type of contract will you be offering?
- What is the allocated budget?

With this information, you can design the functions, responsibilities, and objectives of each worker in your staff to be hired at each position and their short-, medium-, and long-term needs and the places where they will carry out their work, among other aspects.

Candidates' Selection

Make the offer for the interested parties to send their respective curriculum vitae as long as they meet the requested profile. Sometimes the company has the initiative to carry out an internal selection of the personnel it requires. It depends on whether they can meet the demands of the new position. If so, they can take it as a worker promotion. In either option, you need to review each résumé thoroughly. In the end, you can call the selected ones for an interview in the HR department. With this process, you can know the candidates and, in most cases, put them to the test to verify their knowledge and experiences. Thus, those who are considered most suitable for the requested position can be selected.

Staff Recruitment

When the selection process is completed and the right person has been found for the required position, organize thorough paperwork and administrative task for their hiring. All this may imply obtaining extra information from the workers, contract signing, and incorporation into insurance and other economic and social benefits.

When a worker begins his/her functions in a company, he is likely to feel fear, uncertainty, and doubts. There is nothing that reinforces self-confidence better than an affective and effective welcome. The induction process provides positive results since the worker's corporate identity bond with the company begins. The induction time is invested so that the employees know their workplace, the organizational climate and the culture of the company, mission, vision, values, objectives, and commitments. It is the ideal opportunity to meet some of the coworkers, plan upcoming activities, and clarify any doubts.

Education and Training

Once the entire induction process is completed, the worker goes to his place of work to carry out his position, and it may require special education and training so that he knows the objectives and responsibilities. Subsequently, there is planning about training and updating courses, technological advances, and general training, which allow the employees to obtain the necessary experience and help them climb positions in the structure of the organization. You can also offer your workers other activities that can keep them motivated.

Remuneration

Remuneration is an important aspect for employees and the company, that is, the management of payroll and staff benefits with their corresponding deductions. It refers to adequate and equitable compensation for staff to feel motivated and is reflected in their productivity and includes compensations, bonuses, benefits, other economic benefits, vacation periods, days off, and holidays, among others. The HR department is responsible for all these aspects.

Professional Performance Evaluations

Each company has its evaluation mechanism, which allows knowing the level of staff's productivity and other aspects such as punctuality, initiatives, commitment, labor relations, and fulfillment of objectives, among others. The results of these evaluations lead to promotions or demotions.

Staff Motivation

You must promote the degree of motivation in your staff to develop a sense of belonging to your company. Therefore, it is recommended that you develop a special motivation program that encourages your workers to be productive and punctual within their work environment. When you motivate your employees, they automatically feel important, and their thinking focuses on what is being valued and what part of the future of the company is in their hands, which makes them work with greater responsibility, commitment, and satisfaction.

You must understand that no matter how big you are in your company, you will achieve nothing alone; you need a complete team that you can lead. So keep your ego lower. Be humble and understand how important these workers are to you. Thus, you need to understand the importance of your employees and tell them how important they are. The following tips will help you motivate your team:

- Share the benefits of success for the company and the employees.
- Set goals because knowing that they have to achieve something in a specific time motivates them.
- Create healthy competition within the team. You could try to reward the employee of the month.
- It is evident that financial motivation brings good results, so be fair with payments.
- Be friendly with them.
- Ensure a comfortable work environment in terms of treatment, companionship, and physical space.
- Show them the results of their efforts.

On the whole, effective staff management allows your staff to

- be productive at work,
- feel motivated and develop a sense of belonging,
- fully comply with commitments and responsibilities,
- promote and maintain a good working environment,
- desire constant training and education,
- propose ideas,
- be creative and proactive.

Organizational Development

As a health-care entrepreneur, you must know that everyone and everything in your business is important for further development. And here, we are particularly talking about organizational development. In this regard, there is one specific person, that is, the business administrator—the compass of an organization.

Organizational development is the procedure that allows you to organize the resources of your business and utilize them to obtain the highest efficiency and productivity. And for its management to be successful, you must fulfill a series of functions, such as planning, direction, control, organization, coordination, and evaluation of each of the processes. And a business administrator is able to plan, direct, control, organize, and coordinate throughout the process to fulfill these responsibilities and tasks. Thus, these professionals use their knowledge, experiences, strategies, capacities, and negotiation skills to carry their duties. At the end of the day, their objectives allow the business to fulfill its mission and vision.

Depending on the company, the administrative area may be made up of one or more administrators who, in most cases, are the guarantors of the normal development of economic and administrative operations. For organizational development, you need to focus on the following areas when you appoint people for this purpose.

Comprehensive Training

Ideally, they should have knowledge and mastery in countless areas related to management in general, which may include economics, accounting, statistics, logistics, marketing, finance, taxes, management, psychology, ethics, mathematics, social responsibility, and labor legislation, among others. These and other aspects are essential when planning goals, analyzing environments and indicators, solving problems, making decisions, and proposing new strategies.

Teamwork

Undoubtedly, all professionals in all companies, even those who work in groups, in any type of activity and place must learn to work as a team to achieve common objectives and strategic goals. Thus, you must know how to manage your members correctly and delegate functions efficiently. Also, surround yourself with professionals who share the same objectives and responsibilities. Working as a team results in group satisfaction and achieving the set goals.

Managerial Leadership

When we talk about satisfactory teamwork, a leader needs to support, direct, and stimulate his/her group, although it is not an easy process sometimes. Thus, qualified professionals know it all and can control with total authority, understanding specific situations.

Motivator and Trainer

Be a motivator and educator for the benefit of the members of your work team. To do this, you must be a good listener. The percentage of productivity of the employees is not the same; some do not have the same training, disposition, or knowledge. Therefore, the leader or the business administrator must have the ability to motivate his/her team members so that they can work with more encouragement and satisfaction.

Foolproof Strategist

You must also be analytical, observant, critical, and methodical since these characteristics allow you to consolidate your strategic capacity. In this way, you can direct management, a unit, or a department in a more successful way; minimize risks; and increase the probability of success in the programs to be undertaken.

Adaptability

Changes constantly take place in the business world; some are positive and others negative, and some are sudden. So you must always be ready to face these situations with the best disposition and pertinent action in each case. And this demands the ability to adapt and come up with plan B.

Creativity

Creativity should not only be linked to the creation of specific ideas, processes, or actions but it must also be related to the ability to detect solutions and business opportunities that can allow you to achieve your objectives.

Technical Skills

They allow the successful use of knowledge, techniques, procedures, and equipment. Thus, they are essential for the development of responsibilities, commitments, and objectives that can be enhanced through study, training, and experience.

Human Skills

They are about having the capability and will to share and work with a heterogeneous staff and accept and understand their attitudes, feelings, and motivations.

Conceptual Skills

They are the skills to understand the diversity of the company at a general level and the conduct of the personnel within the organization with a view to address the business objectives and needs of the work teams. To ensure successful development, take into account the following areas:

Planning: The process starts with planning since objectives, processes, projects, goals, and everything related to the mission and vision of the company are planned first.

Direction: It is being in charge of channeling orders, instructions, and decision-making with the mission of achieving the success of the administrative, managerial, and productive processes.

Control: It is about monitoring and inspection of the processes.

Organization: Through a well-structured manual, the corresponding responsibilities, functions, and coordination are established.

Coordination: It is about creating a good environment for everyone to work in a coordinated way to get better results.

Control the Time: When you don't learn to properly manage your time, you can lose it between meaningless meetings, which affects overall productivity.

Focus on Planned and Timely Results: Leaders must have the habit of working on specific, measurable, achievable, realistic, and traceable (SMART) objectives.

Create Solid Teams: It is about fostering synergy among all members. Effective leaders exploit the strengths of each team member to achieve great results.

Sense of Priorities: You need to focus on what's important first.

Decide Correctly and Timely: To make effective decisions, follow the correct steps in the correct sequence.

Upgrade: Your biggest challenge is to stay updated. Thus, never stop learning.

Styles of Leadership in Business

When you are in an organization, it is important to identify the leadership styles in business. All companies have one or more leaders who motivate their entrepreneurial team to work toward the achievement of the planned objectives. And the interesting thing is that not all leaders are the same. When you know different styles of leadership, you can specify your performance and your level of communication with your work team in your organization.

A leader is a person who has the talent, training, and tools necessary to be able to influence others, especially those who work on his/her team. Thus, a leader guides, motivates, and directs them to the point of achieving common goals. For the influence to be adequate and successful, the leader needs to have certain characteristics that will allow them to achieve their tasks with effectiveness, precision, ease, and success. The leaders work with respect and honesty to their principles, which is important for their leadership to be recognized by their followers. Thus, they earn the trust and creativity of all those who support, respect, and admire them. In addition, they obtain job satisfaction, know how to adapt to changes in the environment, and achieve continuous improvement of their work, their team, and the company.

Since being a leader has its advantages, the vast majority want to be identified as one of them. However, not everyone has what it takes to be a leader. As a health-care entrepreneur, you must recognize your capabilities to become a leader, and this section will explain them all.

Leadership is about a series of characteristics that make leaders different and that attract and stimulate people/employees to follow them. Before we move to characteristics, let's see what styles are there and how one can develop them.

Autocratic Leadership

These leaders are identified as individualists and extremists. They make decisions without consulting their work team as they feel absolute power over their employees, who only have to obey. They decide quickly without explaining how and why things are done.

They are often described as unpleasant people since they retain their authority through threats, intimidation, punishment, reward, or force. Consequently, their employees reject them and do not want to work with them. There are levels of staff turnover and absenteeism, even resignations. Around such leaders, there is only fear and mistrust.

Bureaucratic Leadership

They follow their strategies according to academic and professional directions. They are self-taught and read what they need to know to make decisions. On some occasions, it is appropriate as special processes can be planned when and if risks arise.

Laissez-Faire Leadership

They accept and support the decision-making of their employees since they believe in them and consider them worthy. They are absolutely sure of the talents, knowledge, and experiences of their employee, so they support them with the necessary tools and resources.

Charismatic Leadership

It characterizes leaders who motivate and inspire their team with a positive attitude and action. Although they have a strong personality, they are good communicators and keep everyone integrated with the aim of crystallizing goals, innovating projects, and promoting productivity.

Democratic Leadership

Also known as participative leadership, it is distinguished by being participatory. The team members and leader exchange and contribute their viewpoints on organizational points of interest to make the most competent and correct decisions. Thus, employees feel valued and remain enthusiastic. Also, with democratic leaders, employees can develop diverse skills, crystallize projects, and feel motivated to continue working together on new challenges.

Transformational Leadership

It is considered the ideal type since it is a complete leadership style. Everything is combined in their way of acting and promoting (i.e., motivation, authority, experience, knowledge, innovation, inspiration, communication, positivism, and authenticity). As a result, they earn the unconditional support of their team.

What Is the Best Leadership Style?

The leadership style distinguishes a leader when it comes to carrying out his professional work in a company. At times, you can adopt one style; and in certain situations, you can adopt others. It will depend on the company's operation and how the team reacts to certain challenges.

So the best leadership style is decided according to the current business situation. Thus, you must learn to put your knowledge, experiences, and skills into practice for the company's benefit, analyzing the main requirements. As an entrepreneur, you can develop these styles in various situations in modern business administration with your management and commitment.

Leadership Qualities

We all need to form our character since nobody is perfect. Some may need it more than others or in different areas, but we all need some qualities. Leadership is a character in action; if the character is bad, leadership will be bad too. If the character is well formed, leadership will be excellent. So let's see the qualities to be an effective leader.

Responsibility

A leader must be responsible. So if you aspire to establish a big business, you must bear the burdens that come with it, and that is why we talk about character. If you lose your mind, you must have self-control and, above all, commitment to what you assume.

Sobriety

To be a sober person means to be moderate in everything that you do. As an entrepreneur and leader, you must be sober. Sobriety speaks of your prudence and how to act and react in the correct way in any situation. You cannot be saying anything without thinking; think and then speak in all situations. Make decisions without letting yourself be carried away. A sober character will prevent you from making bad decisions or hurting or offending people with your words.

Sharing

Be willing to teach and share. Selfishness does not fit in the arsenal of an entrepreneur leader. Understand that your knowledge will give better results if you share it with your team; after all, they will use it in your projects. That is why you should not refuse to share your knowledge.

Patience

Being a leader sometimes makes you feel that you have the power to be a boss, and feeling this power can be risky if and when you are violent. A leader cannot afford to be violent at all. If you are, it will scare your team, and many will be gone before you know it.

Peacemaker

If there is someone who never wants to have a conflict in your team, it is obviously you. Thus, you must be a peacemaker. When you are informed of a conflict, intervene without delay but not like a boss. Instead, seek peace among your team both in and out of business, though it is not always easy. If you have an organizational problem, it will be reflected within in one way or another. So be a peacemaker.

Communication

Communication is one of the most important attributes of a leader. First, you need to make yourself understood, speak clearly, and have your ideas understood by your team. Second, you must listen to those around you to help and guide them.

Updated

As a leader, you must know things that can contribute to the improvement of the productivity of your team and company. Being updated helps you be creative, timely, professional, and appropriate to your company and team.

Charisma

Charisma allows you to reach everyone and leave a good impression. Though it is an internal attribute, you can develop it since it is important to develop good personal and professional relationships. Being charismatic helps achieve challenges and maintain positive thoughts and attitudes.

Planning

Without clear goals, there can be no benefits; and without objectives, there is no performance. Therefore, the team will not have direction if there is no planning; without vision, nothing is achieved. To be a successful leader, you must know how to plan and execute the operating and productivity strategies in the short, medium, and long terms.

Innovation

With innovation, you can create new and better projects with the support of your team, considering the needs of your target audience. These leadership qualities are useful in your endeavor, but you must be willing to improve your character, and you will see the difference on your path to success.

Be an Effective Leader

You need to define and analyze your priorities to be an effective leader. When setting your priorities, consider different aspects of your life; even when we talk about business, we have to think of our personal life too. Your personal life will influence your business.

There are priorities in your personal life that, when left unattended, will end up affecting your business, so list them and respect them. Once you have order in your life, your business can flow much better. Get organized, establish a schedule to attend to your family and children, attend social events, and so on.

If you do not consider priorities, it is like constructing a building without foundation. For example, a priority might be having the money to pay employees versus the need to buy an AC for your office. What if you buy the AC instead of paying your employee? Logically, they will be upset and stop working. So you must consider first things first.

There are irrelevant things, important things, urgent things, and essential things. As a leader and entrepreneur, set your priorities within these groups.

- First, list your needs; it is everything that requires your attention irrespective of urgency.
- Second, place them all in the group, that is, irrelevant, important, urgent, and essential.

See how easy it is. This way, you know your priorities and can act accordingly. Now make an action plan with strategies to address them.

Lead or Manage?

In commercial organizations, there is little clarity about the difference between being a leader and being a manager. Leading and managing are two different things; it is one thing to run a company and another thing to lead it. Thus, leaders go much further than managers. However, both are necessary, and it is possible that a single person can play both roles, but you must be clear about what both terms mean and how their roles are played.

A leader has the ability to influence others by leading them to carry out activities that ultimately bring them the expected results. A leader drives change and is focused on discovering new and better ways of doing what he or she does. In a company, a leader drives growth, especially at a rapid speed.

A manager has the ability to regulate and control situations in such a way that they remain within a certain established order. In a manager's thinking, there is the conviction that the established rules and processes must be followed as this is how achieving the expected results is guaranteed. Thus, control is one of the key functions of managers.

Leaders	Managers
Focuses on making the company innovative	Manages the company
Makes the company increase its value	Quantifies the value of the company
Takes risks, innovates, and develops new ideas to generate new business opportunities	Is in charge of protecting and maintaining what he/she has
Pays more attention to people, considering them company assets that can innovate, create, and develop new lines of business	Focuses on the business structure
Inspires confidence	Believes he/she is in control and exercises it
Has a long-term perspective and a global vision	Focuses on what happens within the company in the short term, solving day-to-day issues

Today we live in an accelerated way, and it makes a greater difference between being a leader and a manager. The leader realizes that only by adjusting to accelerated changes can one be successful, while the manager wants at all costs to avoid the lack of control that accelerated change generates. This gap needs to be resolved for sustained success and to reconcile both roles. The key is flexibility and adaptation.

Strategies for Improvement

Nobody is perfect, so every day we have something to improve, and your health-care company's productivity is one of those things. You must be committed to the values of both the company and your work team so that everything can go as planned; commitment is a fundamental pillar of further improvement. To improve your company, you must improve your commitment. Being a boss is not doing what you want; it is about committing to a team, a vision, clients, suppliers, and everything that has to do with your business. A greater commitment and responsibility translate into better results.

Increasing productivity depends on details such as financial investments in certain areas of the company and small details that make a difference and are important for the development of daily work like equipment renewal, amenities at the workplace, and so on.

Employee Training

Employee training programs greatly help in increasing productivity at all levels. Generally speaking, employers avoid offering training programs as employees leave the company over time. However, it is worse not to update the professional skills of your staff; if they are not updated, the company loses the capacity for competitiveness in the midst of a world that constantly changes and demands people to evolve over time. Thus, good employers never mind training their teams.

You can also sign a contract with the employees to work for a certain period for offering training programs, especially when it comes to high-value programs. If the worker decides to leave the company before the agreed period, he/she must pay for the training. This way, a well-trained staff that is updated in all the novelties and technologies used for daily work is formed.

Employee Motivation

Motivated employees work more at ease and do more for the company. Therefore, you must ensure that working conditions are adequate and that wages and salaries are competitive. Although achieving this may involve an investment, it will have a positive impact on work productivity. In addition, activities that promote coexistence among workers who must perform team tasks and economic or other incentives, such as travel, are also good ways to increase the productivity of workers. This way, they will carry out the campaigns within the deadlines and collaborate to achieve specific objectives for the company.

Incentives also work well for employee motivation. In incentive programs, you can cover economic and noneconomic aspects. A model of noneconomic incentives is to announce the best employee of the week/month/year. It is a sign of being socially accepted, and it is much better if it is paid.

Organization and Planning

Organizing and planning are essential for improved productivity. Setting deadlines to finish the work is important, but these deadlines must be realistic so that they do not represent a source of unnecessary pressure on workers, nor do they allow them to relax excessively, avoiding unnecessarily prolonging processes. You need to have the departments coordinate so that work flows efficiently. When everything happens at a uniform pace, it allows increased productivity without creating a stressful work environment.

Communication with Customers

Having fluid and constant communication with customers is essential. A phone that rings without anyone answering generates a bad impression. On the contrary, finding yourself on the other side with a friendly voice capable of offering answers and quality attention improves the image of the company, having a direct impact on its success.

Management of Employees' Time

Employees' time must be optimized to the maximum; they should not be wasting time doing tasks that do not correspond to them and that prevent them from doing their work on time. So develop a practical schedule and establish a regular monitoring and reporting system.

CHAPTER 10

Insurance Companies and Other Regulatory Agencies

Everyone should have health insurance? I say everyone should have health care. I'm not selling insurance.

—Dennis Kucinich

Since health-care services are expensive in the United States, not everyone can afford to pay for medical services. A doctor's visit may result in the spending of hundreds of dollars; getting admitted within a particular hospital could mean thousands of dollars being spent in one go. This is where health-care insurance comes in. It provides people with the necessary financial resources to spend on their own health care.

Nearly everyone takes advantage of the health-care insurance system within the United States. It is one of the first rites of passage that one has to earn on their way to adulthood. Most people, however, do not realize or invest in the proper kind of investment that suits them personally. To make use of the correct form of investment, you need to know what health-care insurance really is and how and what health-care insurance companies do.

Health-care insurance serves to provide certain financial benefits to those people who have incurred some form of risk that has led to medical expenses. The process consists in you paying a certain premium to any insurance company that provides you with the opportunity to share risk with other people who are also paying the company the same premium. Since not everyone gets sick or injured, the insurance company reserves the right and the responsibility to cover their expenses. Insurance companies are in charge of collecting data over the years to make an estimate of how many people actually need this insurance. They calculate the premium and charge their clients accordingly.

To figure out the best insurance plan, you have to answer certain questions. You need to be clear regarding where you plan to receive care. Since many insurance companies are in touch with specific providers in the chosen areas, they will only provide insurance if that very provider is the one you go to at the time of injury or illness. These providers then present to you a plan that is far more affordable than any other. If you plan on going to other providers, you will be charged a much higher cost than if you are to go to a chosen provider.

You also need to go over the specificities of the particular insurance plan and be clear on what it provides and what it doesn't. Under the Affordable Care Act, you should receive the following essential services:

- Emergency services
- Hospitalization
- Laboratory tests
- Maternity and newborn care
- Dealing with mental health issues and addictions
- Care that is received outside a hospital
- Services that include dental and vision
- Prescription drugs
- Preventive services
- Rehabilitation

If you subscribe to a health-care plan that doesn't come under this act, it will be beneficial to go over what you should ideally be receiving.

Another important thing to note is how much the insurance will cost. The premium is not the only cost that you will have to cover. Paying a small amount for the premium means paying a larger amount later at the point of receiving care. If one pays a larger amount in the beginning, one will have to pay a smaller amount later. These payments come under coinsurance, deductibles, or copays.

Components of Health-Care Insurance

The following are the major components of a health-care insurance plan.

Premium

Premium is the amount you pay to your insurance provider to make sure you receive all the benefits mentioned in the insurance policy. Insurance providers usually categorize you into particular groups based on age or even medical history, which helps them decide the amount of premium you will pay; this, in turn, makes it possible for you to pay equal to or less than the amount you have paid for your premium upon incurring any injury or illness.

Deductible

This is the amount you have to pay before the insurance providers become liable to incur the rest of the cost of your medical care. The premium usually decreases as the deductible increases.

Copay

Not everyone deserves medical attention. It is very easy for people to exploit the medical services and leeway provided by insurance providers. This is the reason behind the existence of an amount of money that you have to pay in addition to the insurance company paying for your medical expenses.

Coinsurance

Insurance companies usually agree on a percentage that they will be paying for the policyholder. Any medical costs will be divided between the policyholder and the insurance company within a particular ratio.

Specificities Not Paid For

Before signing any insurance agreement, you need to be confident regarding what they provide to you and what they don't. Most insurance plans, for example, don't cover body modification. That one will have to be paid out of your own pocket.

Financial Limits

Certain limits are set when it comes to the amount that an insurance company is liable to pay for your medical expenses. Insurance companies don't have an unending limit. Thus, you need to be extremely careful regarding what you are signing up for and the set limit.

Health-Care Insurance in the United States

The United States operates under a system of health care that is unlike any other. Most systems that are observed around the world are centralized and within the control of the government. These systems are universal, and every citizen in the country receives basic health-care services or facilities. Everyone in the United States, however, is not receiving basic health care.

The U.S. health-care system is influenced by a number of elements, such as the political party that rules the country, the economy, the level of technological progress, the condition of the society they operate in, and the general demographic. There are certainly unique qualities and characteristics that set the United States apart from other countries, and we have discussed them in detail in chapter 2.

Issues within Health-Care Insurance in the United States

The United States invests a large amount of money into medicine each year. For them, medicine is a business of sorts. Expenditures on health services and technology have increased tenfold since 1980. It now costs them more than $2.6 trillion a year. This is more than what any other nations spend on their medical systems. Why is it, then, that the United States lags behind when it comes to the provision of health services?

As discussed previously, United States has a privatized system through which they operate, unlike other nations that rely on a centralized system.

This results in people under sixty-five having to pay for their own health care through private insurance companies, which they can access through their employer. Despite the provision of Medicare to those above sixty-five years of age and the provision of private insurance, about 16 percent of the population doesn't receive health-care insurance. This includes fifty million Americans, out of which eight million are children. This is deadly as they are less likely to receive care. Things like cancer can't be diagnosed without screening, and early diagnosis is key to recovery.

Even though insurance is provided to 84 percent of the population, if one compares it with the rest of the world, it is simply not enough. Most of the money goes to copayments and deductibles, and there are many procedures that insurance doesn't cover. Moreover, poor children and communities such as those of Latinos and others simply don't have access to health care.

The average costs of procedures in the United States are higher than those in other countries. Statistics quote an appendix operation costing $13,123 in the United States. Canada's $3,810 paint a bleak picture for the United States' health-care system.

Other problems include but are not limited to

- shortage of medical staff,
- lack of sleep among staff,
- hospital mistakes leading to contamination,
- the question of morality within medicine.

Challenges Faced by Health-Care Professionals

Keeping up with government regulations

The health industry dealt with insurance in an entirely different manner before the Affordable Care Act. Executives in this industry need to be vigilant regarding any governmental regulations or acts that could change the way insurance is paid and what services are included within it. This could lead to complications or even opportunities that executives could make use of in the future.

Making use of big data

Executives need to make sure they have consent before making use of any kind of data within any technological advancement. The information of patients can't be used for any other purpose than the one disclosed to them upon receiving information. This puts executives in a hard place as they can't make use of this sensitive information to figure out the premium that people should pay to insurance providers or even the kind of technology in demand.

Cybersecurity

As medical professionals and entrepreneurs become more and more comfortable with the internet, they are at greater risk of cyberattacks. The occurrence of different kinds of cyberattacks is increasing as the days go by. Online record keeping is becoming more and more common, and a vast amount of valuable data is at risk. Cybersecurity is, thus, worth investing in.

The increased cost of health care

The cost of an annual family plan has gone beyond $20,000 per year. Employers are slowly shifting the cost to employees as technological advancements are introduced to the population.

The increased cost of special drugs

Americans can no longer afford health care that has specifically increased in cost. According to research, these special drugs cost fifty times more than traditional drugs.

What Is Medicaid?

Medicaid was created in 1965 and has since been a dedicated provider of health care to low-income families and individuals. This includes children, adults, and senior citizens. Since it is administered by the federal government and the state, it varies from state to state. In 2018, health coverage was provided to ninety-seven million low-income Americans over one year. Medicaid has been providing services to thirty-two million children, six million seniors, twenty-eight million adults, and nine million people with some form of disability. Medicaid is often mixed up with Medicare, which is also federally administered but is exclusively for people over sixty-five and for some others with disabilities.

Medicaid also changes with the flow of the economic cycle and in the economy. As the economic cycle hits a recession or a slump, people start to lose jobs and even lose out on insurance due to an inability to pay premiums. This is where Medicaid comes in. They provide to those people who can't provide for their own selves.

Eligibility for Medicaid

Certain people fall under the vast umbrella of Medicaid. They are as follows.

- Children lesser than eighteen years of age within families that have an income that is below 138 percent of the poverty line on a federal level
- Women who are pregnant and fall below 138 percent of the poverty line on a federal level
- Any parent or guardian who falls below the poverty line
- Seniors or people who live with disabilities
- People who exist within the groups mentioned above whose income exceeds mandatory coverage limits
- Seniors or those with disabilities who do not receive SSI
- People in special need of medical assistance or those who spend a lot on medical care, such as those in nursing homes

Who Is Not Eligible for Medicaid?

- Adults over twenty-one
- Adults whose income exceeds 42 percent of the poverty line
- Non-U.S. citizens

What Does Medicaid Provide?

- Hospital and physician care
- Laboratory and X-ray tests

- Services provided at home
- Nursing for adults
- Early and periodic screening and diagnostic and treatment benefit for children under twenty-one years of age
- Prescription drugs
- Extra services such as dental care, vision services, hearing aids, and so on

What Is Medicare?

Medicare is a health insurance program delivered by the federal government usually for people over sixty-five years of age.

Eligibility for Medicare

- People who are sixty-five or older
- Some younger people with disabilities or any health issue

What Does Medicare Provide?

- Hospital stays
- At-home care
- Doctor's visits
- Medical tests and X-rays
- Medical supplies and preventive care
- Prescription drugs, dental, vision, hearing aid, fitness regimens

Managed Care Organizations

These are a kind of health insurance organization. They are forever in touch with certain health-care providers and medical facilities to provide care for those members who can benefit from reduced costs. Plans that don't offer you much will have low costs. Plans that are more flexible are usually costlier.

Health Maintenance Organizations

They only pay for health care that falls within their network. You first tend to choose a primary care provider who goes through your medical history and logs your health-care details. This doesn't cover out-of-network services. To avail of this, you will have to live within the network of a particular provider.

Preferred Provider Organizations

These are usually those organizations that pay more if you avail health care within their network. However, they are liable to pay a partial amount if you go outside the network.

Point of Service

These kinds of plans allow you to choose between a health maintenance organization or a preferred provider organization every time you need some form of health care. A managed care plan is basically a system that manages the health-care services for a population that is already enrolled.

Exclusive Provider Organization

These kinds of plans within a managed care system also only work if you go to a provider within the network of a system. A managed care organization is basically a particular organization that is responsible for financing, insurance, and billing of the provision of health-care services. A fixed premium is negotiated between the policyholder and the managed care organization per the health services within the contract. The same organization then works as the insurance company, collecting premiums from the policyholders. The managed care organization then arranges all the services that the providers, hospitals, or clinics need to provide within a contract. There are two ways medical providers are reimbursed, usually through a monthly payment or a schedule of fees.

Billing, Coding, and Reimbursements

What providers do is basically a documentation of some important details that pertain to the patient's history and the medical problem being presented. Through this, they can get to a particular conclusion regarding the particular diagnosis and plan. All this goes into medical records for ease of access.

The electronic health record exists for the convenience of service providers. The assignment of medical codes makes it easy for anyone to understand what documentation basically means. The codes translate difficult information into concise terms, which are then used by payers to understand what service is being performed and why. The provider will submit these codes to the software, followed by a claim submission. Payers will then review these claims before applying for health-care reimbursement. Each service has a particular rate attached to it that takes into consideration practice and malpractice expenses. The more the services being provided, the more the payment received.

Hospitals are usually paid based on something called diagnosis-related groups that allot fixed amounts for each hospital stay. Spend less than this, and you make a profit. Spend more, and you make a loss.

Other Regulatory Agencies

Bodies that are responsible for regulation within the United States health-care system may include private or public entities that work at the federal or state and city levels. Major federal regulatory organizations include the following:

- CMS
- CDC
- FDA

All of them fall under the U.S. Department of Health and Human Services. State regulatory bodies include the following:

- Public health departments
- Provider licensing boards
- Insurance commissioners

There exists some independent nongovernment health provider organizations, mainly AMA and the Joint Commission, which are separate regulators in the health-care system.

CHAPTER 11

Cash Flow, Revenue Management, and Return on Investment

The value of a business is a function of how well the financial capital and the intellectual capital are managed by the human capital. You'd better get the human capital part right.
—Dave Bookbinder

Cash Flow

For a business to operate with stability and achieve objectives, it is necessary to always have a clear financial standing. It depends on the financial analysis and cash flow and how it affects the company's decisions. Understanding cash flow is important in the short-, medium-, and long-term plans and projects of the business.

Cash flow is a financial report that presents details of the income and expenditure of a company. It records every financial activity; and it includes income from sales, debts, loans, salaries, rent, payment of bills, taxes, and interests, among others. Thus, cash flow is the entry and exit movement of the money generated by the company in a given period. The flow of money represents the accumulation of liquid assets of a company.

Be clear about the difference between income and expenses. If this balance is positive, it means that the inflows of money during a certain period are higher than the expenses. The negative balance suggests that the expenses of the company are greater than the income. In other words, cash flow is the fundamental indicator of income and expenses.

Cash flow from operating activities

It is about the entry and exit of money to the organization as a result of its movements or commercial activities such as income from product sales or service provision and expenses for agreements with suppliers, among others.

Cash flow from financing activities

It has to do with the money that comes in and goes out either for debts or issuance of shares or for the cancellation of profits to the company's shareholders.

Cash flow from investing

It is the money that comes in and goes out, depending on the investments made by the company with the purpose of improving its functions, operations, and productions. They are positive investments that, when canceled, are transformed into liquidity.

Managing cash flow is important because it is the first factor to be considered to determine a company's growth in addition to the profitability of the commercial actions carried out. For this, the ROI must be mentioned, a financial indicator that allows you to measure the profitability of an investment. In turn, knowing the cash flow allows you to anticipate eventualities in the market and minimizes the risks of possible debts. Also, cash flow is perfect for increasing the appeal of your company for investors as it provides statistics on the functionality and profitability of the project, which every investor wants to know.

Regarding the operation of the company, the cash flow allows you to respond to the following:

- How much merchandise can you buy from suppliers?
- What type of merchandise is the most requested by customers?
- Is it convenient to implement a credit payment strategy?
- Can you invest surpluses in new projects?

- How much cash does the company have?
- How many more staff members can you hire?

These aspects are the basis for the proper functioning of any business as they help in anticipating certain market behaviors according to the consumption habits of users in a certain period. Also, they allow measurement of profits (or losses) of the executed marketing and advertising strategies.

Maintain cash flow because it is also a legal requirement to determine the treasury charges and other taxes that the organization must pay. Therefore, organize, update, and keep the accounting book. Having these instruments up to date and in order will facilitate the process of calculating cash flow. Cash flow is calculated in certain periods, usually at the end of each month, and the collection of this data allows projection of the company's financial future. Cash flow is the best of allies for any investment project. If you are a start-up and you are looking to attract investors, do not take it for granted to show the statistics of the financial year of your company.

Accounting books are used to maintain cash flow. They are the documents wherein all financial information of a company is recorded. Accounting books are periodically updated. When a new fiscal year begins, new ledgers are also created. Traditionally, the information is reflected on paper; with the rise of new technologies, many companies have started to use accounting books in digital format.

The most common accounting books are the following.

Daybook

All operations carried out by the company are recorded in the daybook. It is configured as a succession of accounting entries, arranged chronologically.

Inventory Book

It includes all the accounts with the company's balance, such as assets, liabilities, net worth, expense, and income, and it is periodically updated. The last balance must coincide with the balance sheet made for the annual accounts. In addition, the inventory book must include the opening balance and the inventory, that is, the physical units that make up the company's inventory and their valuation.

Annual Reports

They reflect the economic-financial information of the company. They consist of five documents (i.e., balance sheet, income statement, statement of changes in equity, cash flow statement, and memory). They are drawn up once a year.

Ledger

They represent a summary of all ledger accounts. It has all the movements that affect the debit and credit of the corresponding account. The balance is the difference between the debit and the credit. We can also maintain a bankbook that reflects bank movements and a cashbook that reflects cash movements (i.e., payments and collections).

Revenue Cycle Management

As a health-care entrepreneur, you need to ensure that your business follows a successful process to stay financially healthy. And you can do it with health-care revenue cycle management (RCM), an overarching blend of claims processing, payment, and revenue generation. RCM is a financial circulatory system of a health-care business. It comprises administrative and clinical functions to capture, manage, and collect patient service revenues; in short, RCM represents the whole life of a patient's account. Thus, it manages functions related to claims processing, payment, and revenue generation, encompassing the identification, management, and collection of patient service revenue.

RCM starts working as soon as a patient is given the appointment for obtaining medical services, and it is completed at collecting all payments. However, it is not as easy as it sounds. When a patient is given an appointment, the staff manages scheduling, insurance eligibility, and the establishment of the patient's account.

The following areas need to be covered to create an effective RCM:

- Scheduling or preregistration
- Point-of-service registration counseling collection
- Utilization review and case management

- Charge capture and coding
- Claim submissions
- Third-party follow-up
- Remittance processing and rejections
- Payment posting, appeals, and collections

As an entrepreneur, you can focus on the following areas in the RCM.

System Integration

The RCM can be siloed, leading to lost revenue opportunities. You can examine integrated software and hardware systems that can help in combining patient accounting, billing, collections, and electronic health records.

Billing and Claims Management

You can focus on the following areas:

- Reduce denials and rejected claims
- Train staff on denial management processes
- Improve point-of-service collections
- Lessen delays in patient billing
- Improve revenue cycle productivity

Contact Analysis

When you have strong data and strategy, it can help a health-care organization leverage negotiation. Other areas include coding/ICD-10 and clinical documentation demands. When you understand the parts of a complex RCM, you can break down the whole processes, observe weaknesses and improve them, and make sure that you collect maximum revenue for the services you deliver.

Though the RCM is a great way to manage the whole cycle, there are certain challenges. Since changes occur in health-care regulations and reimbursement models, a health-care organization may find it hard to maintain its stability regarding RCM policies and practices. One particular challenge is to collect payments from patients at or before the point of service.

Though the collection of payments before a patient leaves the office is time saving, it is observed as a difficult task, whereas collecting at point of service is harder because many patients don't have the capacity to pay upfront.

Another challenge is to track claims through their life cycle. A health-care professional needs to monitor claims processes to pinpoint if and when errors occur. If errors are not pinpointed timely along with their origins, it can cause financial losses to providers. To solve this issue, automated alerts and staff training can work well. Staff training will also help in reducing human errors like improper coding and insurance eligibility problems.

Return on Investment (ROI)

Investing money requires keys to its best performance. If you already have a long experience as an entrepreneur or a successful professional or have inherited investments, you may have a considerably positive cash flow. When we invest, we do it to generate a better return on investment. ROI is a financial indicator that allows you to measure the profitability of an investment in the company. By measuring ROI, you can determine the percentage of profit on a given investment.

It is the indicator of the profits that have been obtained after carrying out certain actions. With ROI, you can calculate the conversions and the results obtained from a specific investment. Measuring these results allows you to visualize the performance of your work and detect failure or improvements to amortize the investment made.

However, you always have to be alert. Many people say that when it comes to entrepreneurship, you have to be an expert in numbers, calculations, and metrics. If not an expert, you do need to learn about ROI, and we will go through it in this section.

ROI shows you in numbers if the objectives in terms of production, sales, and distribution are being met. The process includes reviewing metrics, performing calculations, and examining the results of business strategies. Therefore, it is important that you are aware of what ROI is like.

One of the most important benefits of knowing ROI is that you have the possibility to determine if the investment you are making is profitable or not and in what percentages. Thus, you can make the worthy ones and find out how to improve others. The ROI is ideal for calculating the profitability levels of the organization's investments regarding production, distribution, and services, among others. The ROI serves to

- measure the performance of an investment,
- calculate the efficiency of expenses,
- facilitate budget optimization,
- improve decision-making,
- control marketing campaigns and investments.

To calculate ROI, the time variable must be taken into account. There is a simple formula that allows you to measure the profitability of the investment. The calculation of ROI is as follows.

The cost of the investment is subtracted from the current value of investment and then divided by the cost of the investment. Since ROI is expressed as a percentage, the result is multiplied by 100 to get a final percentage.

$$ROI = \frac{\text{Current Value of Investment} - \text{Cost of Investment}}{\text{Cost of Investment}}$$

Example

Suppose you invested $100,000 in a business, and you got sales of $250,000. So you have the following numbers:

$$\frac{250,000 - 100,000}{100,000} = 1.5$$

$$1.5 \times 100 = 150\%$$

If the ROI is not positive, it means that it is not advisable to make the investment. If the ROI is equal to zero, it means that the profit is equal to the expenses.

By using this formula, you can calculate the profitability of any type of financial investment strategy. Therefore, measure the profitability to determine the profitable options.

CHAPTER 12

Growth Strategy

Incredible things in the business world are never made by a single person, but by a team.

—Steve Jobs

Your journey to success will not end with the establishment of your health-care business; in fact, it is just the beginning since you have to grow bigger and bigger. So it is time to work on your growth strategy. To make an effective growth strategy, you need to understand and focus on the four stages of a product's life cycle.

With creation comes an end, right? In short, a cycle is the close union of two extremes, whose route can be short or long, depending on the perspective with which it is seen or the objective it meets. The stages of the life cycle of a product are as follows:

- Introduction
- Growth
- Maturity
- Decline

Life Cycle of a Product

The life cycle of a product is the number of sales that an item has during the time it is on the market. It translates into the stages through which a product passes on the market, from its introduction to its decline. These stages occur with different periods, and each one depends on its promotion, competition, and demand, among other aspects; and finally, they are determined by consumers as judges and main critics of that product.

The duration of each stage can vary from minutes, days, weeks, years, and even centuries. It can depend on various factors such as the product category, consumer trends, technology, marketing campaigns, and the level of acceptance by consumers.

Introduction

It is the first and the most important stage since it is the presentation of the product, the moment when the public gets to see the product for the first time. You will have successfully passed the first step if people say, "I'm going to try it." However, there are cases when a product appears and gets slow sales. If it happens, don't panic; at this stage, you need to keep working on making your product known and find new consumers. The slope is high, but it can be climbed. So observe your target audience or consumers' reaction and how the product can meet their needs more efficiently. You may also have to play with the price and do tests. The receptivity of the consumer will depend on the characteristics of the product, uses, satisfaction of needs, and quality. And always measure the results, and only then can you adapt.

To meet the needs of the market and consumers, you must be careful, especially when it comes to technological products. At the beginning of this process, everything is fascinating for the novelty of the idea and the product. When the novelty is in full swing in its promotional stage, all looks great. Since there is an audience that follows and loves everything new and in fashion, the product is initially sold for emotional reasons rather than rational. If you focus on the emotional, you will have to make a great effort to change "emotions" while being a practical and rational product; it can fall under its own weight.

Growth

This stage starts when the product has been accepted; its sales, benefits, and demand increase; and the overall market expands. In this phase, companies usually maintain prices and quality while they decide to expand their distribution process to other markets based on analysis of a previously carried out market study. At this stage, you want to project your production. Moreover, sales multiply because you are sort of monopolizing or dominating the market. However, you still may not know the potential of your product, so don't think that these sales are due to factor A or B. Instead, you should wait for the sales to hit the ceiling and analyze later. Simply, keenly observe, analyze, and promote with caution. With this data, you can see how well accepted and responsive your product is to real consumers' needs.

While growing upward, certain things show deficiencies that will manifest at some point. As you are growing with the product, you come across an obstacle like a wall. You can't help it, and you crash into this wall. You solve the problem, grow back, and then crash again. It sort of becomes a continuous process. You grow and crash and repeat. The possible reasons include support or distribution capacity and cost reduction if competitors emerge or other adverse circumstances arise and internal financial problems. To face it, the human and technological capacity of resources needs to be increased for growth.

Maturity

At this stage, competition appears, and the demand no longer grows, and it is highly likely that products with similar names and characteristics start appearing in the market. It is like a stagnation stage as the sales are maintained for a while without making additional efforts since the product already has acceptance. And this is when you start to see the saturation of the market, and a drop in sales is expected. You can introduce a new version of your product to keep your customers interested in your product.

Decline

At this stage, attraction, sales, and profitability fade or may fall flat since your consumers begin to consume other products that meet their needs. In short, there is more variety on the market. When it happens, some companies may decide to sell the product at reduced prices until it is time to divest. Others think of modifying the features that could help in keeping the product on the market for a while longer.

For effective growth strategies, you need to start taking steps in view of the life cycle of your product. You just have to locate what stage you are in and apply the relevant strategies along with other general growth strategies discussed below.

Preventing Obvious Mistakes

It is true that we can learn from mistakes, but there are some that we don't need to make to learn. In other words, you can learn from others' mistakes.

Be Clear

If you aren't sure where you want to go or what you are going to do to get there, it will be difficult for your business to prosper. Thus, have a clear vision and well-planned short-term and long-term goals. Have it all on paper because only then will you be able to work based on what you want to achieve.

Passion

Passion is not just to talk about something beautiful but passion has also shown that it is the key to success in many businesses. So fall in love with what you do, work hard, and do it in the best possible way. Your attitude when it comes to entrepreneurship has a lot to do with success.

Discipline

You can have a phenomenal business growth strategy, but if you don't implement it as it should be with discipline, it won't work. If someone asks you how to grow your business, simply answer that you must discipline yourself. To do things with discipline, avoid working the hours you want; instead, set a schedule and stick to it and be responsible to yourself.

Work as a Team

Teamwork has been the key to business success for entrepreneurs as well as seasoned businesspeople. It is a grave mistake if you believe that you don't need help. The following points work best to work as a team:

- Partner with someone to undertake
- Hire people to work with you
- Establish relationships with other businesses to strengthen yours

Automate and Optimize

Time is a very important factor in the life of health-care entrepreneurs. Knowing how to use time correctly means that you can do more in less time, which can be translated into higher production, growth, and more income. And this is where we talk about automation and optimization. In terms of product manufacturing processes, you need to find a way to produce more in less time. It is not about buying expensive machinery only but about something as simple as proper organization. There are times when you may produce less just because of poor organization. Thus, observe and analyze what you can do to optimize and automate the different activities in your business regarding product development, paperwork, and customer service, among others.

Reinvest

Investment is what you make in the beginning, but you must always do it to grow the business as well, and reinvestment works in this regard. The reason many businesses fail is that the profits are spent. The right thing to do is always have a percentage to invest in something or someone to grow your business. To grow your business, you must grow, develop, and in many cases extend through reinvestment. You are not supposed to spend all the profits; consider a percentage to reinvest and build a solid and successful business.

Use Digital Media

A few years ago, having a fan page about your business was something innovative. Today it has become essential. However, don't settle for having a social network page; you must cover all digital media. Thus, you have to have more than one social network and ensure that you make a good digital presence. Also, ensure that it grows every day and has interaction with people. In short, it is about being everywhere and even paying for advertising to appear on third-party sites.

Social Media

Social media networks allow more direct and fluid communication between health-care professionals as well as consumers and patients. Good use of social networks by health-care professionals positively influences their prestige and that of the company they have or in which they work. Also, social media interactions can considerably increase traffic on your website, which ultimately translates into more patients.

Today social media has claimed its place in the business and marketing world. Thus, knowing the social networks that your target audience use is important to know where to focus your digital presence on social media. The most used social media networks today are the following.

Twitter

Twitter is on the way to replacing traditional media. In fact, there is a lot of news that appears on Twitter before any other medium. Its immediacy and the brevity of the tweets make it a great communication tool with your target audience, and in fact, many health organizations already use it to issue health alerts.

Instagram

With eight hundred million users worldwide, Instagram is one of the social networks that have grown the most in recent years. It publishes images and small videos, so in principle, it is relevant in the health sector too. It can particularly be useful for aesthetic clinics, which can show images with the result of their treatments.

YouTube

Although many people view YouTube as a video portal rather than a social network, it also falls into this category. Many health-care services take advantage of this platform to upload explanatory videos of the procedures they perform. Seeing how a professional does their job is a good way to promote yourself and gain the trust of potential clients.

LinkedIn

LinkedIn is designed for job search and professional networking. It is precisely this last function that is the most interesting for health-care entrepreneurs who can make contacts and share information of interest with colleagues and other people. The professional social network is more focused on the relationship and interaction with other specialists as a forum and space for debate with experts in the same field.

Facebook

Facebook continues to lead as the most used social network with a whopping three billion users. So it is the essential place for any health-care company to be. The best way to use Facebook is by creating a fan page where you can share quality content. You can also create a group and link it to the page. This channel is great for promotion and interaction. To get followers on Facebook, take the following steps:

- It is important that communication is bilateral as it generates trust and closeness. Use your Facebook page to clarify minor health-care-related questions to gain a reputation.
- Create content that is easily understandable. The content of the posts must be truthful to respect the idiosyncrasies of health-care information.
- Incorporate visual elements. As in any other field, publications gain value if they incorporate images that illustrate the content. For example, it is positive to publish daily images of specialists offering a viewpoint for users who visit your profile.
- Share posts from other specialists in the field. It is convenient to share articles that can help your followers; it diversifies the

authorship of the content of your account, and you will have more possibilities for other profiles in the sector to share your publications.

- Always include your name or that of the company to build brand awareness and reputation.

Public Relations

Public relations refers to a set of strategies that are part of introducing and marketing to encourage, guide, and measure the reaction of a specific audience with respect to a product/service, a character, a brand, or an organization. Also, it is in charge of representing a brand and is the communication bridge that connects the public with the companies.

Any means of communication is suitable for handling public relations. The secret of each relationship is to find what type of media is to be used for communication strategies that the business needs. Thus, it all depends on the type of information and interaction.

The strategy within PR marketing is the exchange of information and opinions to build references that can promote your business. A reference is a recommendation that your company obtains from an authentic source, and the benefits of associating with a good referral source are unmatched—part of good PR marketing.

Remember that connections are not about the number of business cards you collect during an event or the friends you have on LinkedIn; it is about expanding the circle of people with whom you have quality communication and related interests. To have successful connections, you need to maintain continuous contact with your new connections and have genuine business interests. Common interests can be as simple as sharing mutual information on a particular topic within the industry in which you operate to close joint deals.

Many people find it difficult to make new connections because it involves introducing yourself and selling yourself to a new person. There will be events where you will need to introduce yourself to the same people over and over again, but if you maintain a good PR strategy, you won't have to introduce yourself to random people or forcefully sell the value of your company.

Let other people know what you do and that you are interested in a referential relationship. Many entrepreneurs love to talk about their businesses, but you must ask questions about others' businesses to establish public relations. When you design a PR strategy, explore how elements of persuasive communication are used in this context. These elements are as follows.

What: What do you aspire to do with the contact person?

If you are an ally, it is a good idea to generate a pitch about how your product/service can add value to them. If it is a potential angel investor, the messages should show the potential of the business and the work team.

Who: Who is the brand spokesperson?

Exercise the voice that is carried out by an influential person with total credibility. For example, if your brand is related to organic food, it is natural that the spokesperson is an example of a healthy life.

Where

Specifying the places with all the details is essential. The meeting place should be adequate to gather all those called to that event.

When

The date and time is also important. If there is an unforeseen change, notify immediately the invited parties.

To whom

It is convenient to develop a plan that considers all stakeholders in addition to possible allies, clients, and the media.

How

To talk to important people, design the best way to approach someone and get their attention at that time or on an upcoming date. For example, if you meet a person at a conference, get closer by showing interest in their presentation. Another way is to get a third party who knows both parties.

Channel

You can deliver information through press releases, interviews, and the like. Also, conferences and conventions are key to building a network of a very specific audience.

CHAPTER 13

Burnouts

In dealing with those who are undergoing great suffering, if you feel "burnout" setting in, if you feel demoralized and exhausted, it is best, for the sake of everyone, to withdraw and restore yourself. The point is to have a long-term perspective.
—Dalai Lama

Working toward a better quality of life can be challenging for most. Introduce the health-care sector to the mix, and you have got yourself a recipe for disaster, lest you keep a lookout. Entrepreneurship is a difficult feat to accomplish in itself, and being in the health-care sector can mean burnout for the best of people.

Burnout targets each of its victims uniquely and strategically. It lies dormant till it is least expected and comes out in the worst ways possible. Picture this: You have spent months scouring the internet for the procurement of a specific technology that could lead to the improvement of the lives of the patients who reside within your customer's hospital. Upon receiving it, you start to experience a plethora of symptoms, none of which can be explained. You feel empty, mentally drained, devoid of any happiness that relates to what you have just acquired and so on. This reaches the level where you are left uncaring toward any advancement, no matter what its nature. You are burning out.

Fortunately, burnouts have both a prevention and a cure. Gone are the days when people needed to suffer for days, keeping their work on hold for when they felt better. The future is now.

What Is Burnout?

Herbert Freudenberger first coined the term *burnout* in the 1970s when he was attempting to explain the symptoms felt by most people in the helping profession. This definition was built for people such as doctors and nurses who went through the added pressure of saving lives. Entrepreneurship within the health sector affects many people in a similar way. This sector leads to a high moral compass and an extreme amount of stress, resulting in feelings of exhaustion and an inability to enjoy the fruition of hard work.

This definition has since expanded to include, yet not be limited to, housewives, taxi drivers, corporate workers, and so on. *Burnout* is an umbrella term that encapsulates within itself many definitions and kinds of workers that it affects. This is the reason behind many psychologists and human resource managers not agreeing on the exact definition and causes of burnout. It is a phenomenon that is not researched on, yet it underlies many of the problems faced by any and every worker one might come across.

Once a workplace establishes the fact that burnout exists, it can proceed to differentiate it from general stress or tiredness. One goes through a number of problems in the workplace. Colleagues who just do not get along, a work environment not conducive to growth, feeling as if one is not being pushed toward achieving their optimal level of performance, or even receiving an amount of work that simply cannot be completed within the time allotted—these are just some of the basic reasons why one might feel uncomfortable at work and tread the thin line between routine stress and burnout. Stress can also cause problems at home that are not addressed at work.

Burnouts are psychological in nature, yet their effects are felt physically. The biggest cause of burnout could be attributed to one neglecting their own needs for the well-being of the company. Yet what sets it apart is the consistency of stress being felt at work. If one's levels of stress remain constantly elevated for a long period, so much so that they cannot perform as efficiently as they are able to, one could be facing burnout.

Some telltale signs of burnout include severe exhaustion. This is felt both physically and mentally. It usually happens when one is unable to work or enjoy anything that exists at the workplace. One also feels a lack of energy during this time. Some studies show how these issues lead to stomach problems that put the person in question in ever greater distress. Furthermore, the person stops feeling any form of empathy or compassion toward any of their colleagues. They also feel a sense of not being worth anything, a small cog in a big machine without whom the company will go on working as they have done before—this kind of alienation is unavoidable when one is undergoing this particular level of stress. Research shows burnout to be almost as high as 52 percent among health-care professionals, a whopping 32 percent increase from the 20 percent that teachers, professors, and humanitarian aid workers feel.

So what exactly is the science behind burnout? It all circumambulates emotion. Our nervous system makes us undergo many emotions in a day. Some might be bad and others good; however, as long as one keeps moving, one never hits a roadblock. Problems arise when we tend to get stuck on one emotion. This is particularly the case with health-care workers who have to interact with so many people and organizations in need every day. The decisions they make directly affect the lives of many people in question.

Thus, burnout is a serious problem that seems to mainly affect people in the health-care industry. For one to understand how to control burnout, one needs to understand the causes. This could lead to early prevention of emotional exhaustion. All in all, if one cannot deal with burnout before it occurs, one can at least ponder on the cure. This will eventually lead to a better quality of life for the person in question as well as those who work around him/her.

Causes of Burnout

According to Freudenberger and North, there exist twelve phases of burnout.

- Excessive levels of ambition
- Pushing oneself beyond one's limits
- Not being able to meet one's basic needs
- Blaming others for one's own mistakes
- Time management issues
- Existing in a state of denial
- Withdrawing from society
- Stark changes in behavior
- Feelings of detachment or alienation

- Emotional emptiness
- Depression
- Complete collapse of mental health

One of the main causes behind burnout among entrepreneurs in the health-care sector could be the level of responsibility allotted to these professionals. Emotions are tricky and, if not handled well, can spin out of control. If one is consistently responsible for the health and safety of all their clients, it is hard for them to give themselves leeway for any misadventure. This has to do with the amount of workload one takes on during their time at the workplace. The greater the workload, the greater the anxiety as the chances of disappointing one's clients increase. When one works to the extent of their own capabilities, one seldom gets tired; however, pushing oneself beyond one's natural abilities is a recipe for disaster.

A lack of control could also lead to feelings of despair and exhaustion. When one is an entrepreneur, one seldom needs to ask people for advice. However, if the market is out of control and unpredictable, it won't be a long time before the said entrepreneur feels burdened. Control is one of the many things that humans value above everything else. The second they feel their life is going out of control, they pull on the reins, and everything comes to a halt. This is the same with a workplace environment.

Entrepreneurs in the health-care sector may sometimes fail to acquire particular rewards that they have looked forward to during their business ventures. Perhaps the technology that they are providing is not affordable by small- and medium-sized industries, and due to the existence of a moral compass, they provide it at a lower cost. This means less profit for the businessman. After years of hard work, if the market does not repay what it owes, it could lead to a lack of motivation.

The risk factor when it comes to the health-care sector far outweighs the benefits. The world is changing and along with it the diseases that the world itself introduces. The applications or technology one introduces to combat a particular disease might get obsolete by the time it reaches the market. The amount of hard work that is put into these inventions surpasses that of any other industry. A consistent level of risk will put the entrepreneurs in a stressful situation. This consistent risk could serve to stress them out and exhaust them to the point of no return.

Moreover, in the health-care sector, there is often a clash of values. Whatever one decides to invest in, there are always fallouts. Be it a particular entrepreneur who decides to put their money into the provision of hospice for the elder generation or one who decides to improve the quality of life of the younger generation, both are at fault in the eyes of society. No matter what they choose, the other party loses out.

Avoiding Burnout

To avoid burnout, ask yourself the following questions:

- Where is it coming from?
- What can you do about it at the moment?
- Can you trust someone with it?
- Are there any other options that you can explore?
- Can you make up for the loss of control?
- Can you restrict yourself?
- Are your needs being met?
- Are you happy?
- Do you need to talk to a professional?

The path toward a good life and the avoidance of excessive levels of burnout is answering all the questions listed above.

To prevent burnout, one needs to first analyze where it is coming from. Burnout can be caused by a number of things, and some of which are mentioned above. Recognizing the early signs of burnout is essential toward its prevention. One needs to educate themselves on the reasons that could cause burnout and then keep a lookout for the same.

You also need to ask what you can do about your burnout immediately:

- Can you distance yourself from the situation?
- Can you simply get up and walk away?
- Can you take a meditation break?

Perhaps you have been working on some tasks that you can do without. Delegate them to your partners or employees and focus on what you can do best.

Humans need one-on-one interactions, even at the workplace. Figure out a colleague worthy of trust and speak your heart out. Venting could lead to a dissipation of the beginning phases of burnout, which could prevent it from worsening. If the idea of talking to someone does not call out to you, simply speak to a professional. This could be someone from the HR department or a therapist who could sort out the issues you are facing and help you view them in a better light.

Take time out in the day for yourself. Read a book, exercise, or meditate. Research has proved that exercise and meditation are stress busters of the highest level. If you love yourself, your employees will love your attitude.

Make sure your basic needs are being met—these range from sleep to food and warmth. If one neglects something as basic as sleep, one is in great danger of emotional exhaustion.

Dealing with Burnout

There are some steps you can take to cure emotional exhaustion or to surpass the final levels of burnout.

Admit that you have burnt out

The first stage is to admit that something is wrong. Without admitting that basic fact, you can never improve your quality of life. Some people do not believe that burnout exists. Others do not believe that burnout can affect them. The latter are the kind who pride themselves on not being weak and on being perfectionists. Burnout is not a sign of weakness. It can affect anyone and everyone, and rising above this prejudice will definitely lead to a better quality of life.

Isolate yourself from work

Maybe you just need some time off work. It is never a bad idea to take breaks or even to utilize the benefit of being your own boss. Simply delegate responsibilities and opt out for a couple of days.

Treat yourself with some me time

Read a book, learn an instrument, or get invested in a sport. Vent out your frustration wherever and whenever you can. Exercise or meditate however much you can so that your brain is forever active, not just at your workplace but otherwise too.

Sleep

Make sure your basic needs are met. Without your basic needs, you can never perform at the optimum level.

Helping others

What can you do for someone who is going through the stages of burnout?

- Listen to them
- Make them feel like their problem is valid
- Offer help with work
- Offer other kinds of help
- Make them happy through a gesture
- Connect them with a professional

How to Attain a Better Quality of Life

Maslow's hierarchy of needs did for us what probably no other theory could have done. It presented to each and every person who came in direct contact with it a unique way to live life. Everyone wants to discover the pot of gold at the end of the rainbow. Everyone has that innate desire to improve something about themselves or add something to their life. Yet nobody knows what that really is.

Before diving into the ways to attain a better quality of life, one should focus on the root cause of that quality. This is where Maslow comes in. This hierarchical theory basically revolves around the psychological concept of motivation. Why do people do what they do? What drives them to do particular things and not others? There are five main stages of the model. The first one is physiological need (food and shelter). Then follows safety (some form of job security), the need for love or belonging, self-esteem, and self-actualization, respectively.

Physiological survival focuses on the basic needs that a human being might need to survive in life. This includes food, shelter, clothing, warmth, and sleep. In case these needs are not met, Maslow concluded that they could lead to stunted growth. If these basic needs are ignored, one cannot proceed toward a better quality of life. Entrepreneurs in health care mostly neglect their basic needs, which leads to burnout in most cases. Only when they meet their basic needs can they advance to the next level.

The next level is that of safety. One needs to feel secure in their job. Even a layman knows the fact that entrepreneurship is not void of risk. One wrong move could lead to years of hard work wasted. As mentioned above, any human being wants to feel like they are in control of their lives. No one wants to feel threatened, yet that is exactly the environment that a business gives rise to.

This is then followed by love and the need to belong to a certain place. It is essential for entrepreneurs to have an inner circle that they relate to. Entrepreneurs are like eagles in that they fly alone. They often have to make decisions that distance them from people. This could also be a major cause of burnout. Humans are social animals and thus need to be motivated accordingly.

Esteem needs are also important. They are those needs that revolve around the way you respect yourself and the way others respect you. This rung in the ladder is easy to achieve for entrepreneurs in the health-care department. They are already working for the wellness of many people in society. Additionally, they are automatically respected as entrepreneurs.

The final level, according to Maslow, is that of self-actualization. This occurs when one realizes their true potential. This is where your quality of life is at the optimal level. According to a quality-of-life theory influenced by this hierarchy of needs, developing societies focus more on the lower levels such as food and security, while developed societies tend to focus more on self-actualization. This is the reason behind them having a higher human development index and a better quality of life. This could be extended to entrepreneurs. This quality of life, according to the theory, is measured through need satisfaction. The higher the need satisfaction, the greater the quality of life. Entrepreneurs can focus on meeting these particular needs to experience a fulfilled and optimal quality of life. This will lead to lesser levels of burnout altogether.

Being an entrepreneur is highly challenging, and it, at times, totally drains out your energy. The breaking point for an entrepreneur occurs when the situation turns out to be extremely tense that they think they cannot continue their entrepreneurship further. Thus, they are on the verge of throwing the towel. However, for most entrepreneurs, the ultimate loss of enthusiasm for entrepreneurship, which we know as burnout, is a gradual process. As a result, it starts making a negative impact on their performance at work. I am sure it is a situation that no entrepreneur want to experience. So let me tell you that it is a 100 percent preventable issue.

Burnout for entrepreneurs has devastating effects, which will cause fatigue and despair over time, ultimately making you quit your endeavors. In addition to mental and emotional effects, burnout affects you physically. And the worst part is that these effects multiply if left unattended.

In the above part of this chapter, I have shared burnout reasons and solutions, so just go through them once again and follow them to get rid of your entrepreneurial burnout and keep on moving ahead on the success track.

CHAPTER 14

Mindset—Becoming an Entrepreneur: From Faith to Action

> *Entrepreneur is someone who has a vision for something and a want to create.*
>
> —David Karp

Mindset shapes the lives we lead, the actions we take, and the possibilities of the world we live in. The word *mindset* was first used in the 1930s, which meant "habits of mind formed by previous experience." In simple words, mindsets are deeply held beliefs, attitudes, and assumptions we create about who we are and how the world works.

Mindsets are created from the distinctions we can make about our experiences. We undergo experiences from which we make distinctions. From these distinctions, we create new mindsets.

Mindsets shape our everyday lives. We create our own mindsets, and thereafter, our mindsets create us. Our thoughts, words, and actions are released from our mindsets like ripples on the surface of a lake. If there is something we want to change in our lives, such as being more creative or improving our well-being, we must be open to shifting our mindsets.

The more developed our mindsets become, the more we incline toward more profound levels of wisdom and effectiveness in the world. Our mindsets evolve from simple to complex, from static to dynamic, and from egocentric to socio-eco-centric. Our ability to create a perspective improves with our capacity to embrace ambiguity and hold paradox.

What's inside us—our beliefs, attitudes, and assumptions—manifest outside, shaping our possibilities on both individual and collective levels. In other words, mindsets are a mental inclination, a disposition, or a frame of mind. Your mindset is your collection of thoughts and beliefs that shape your habits and behavior. Your habits and behavior then affect how you think, what you feel, and what you do. It also helps understand attitudes and beliefs. It frames our self-concept (the comprehensive view we have about ourselves).

Mindset—a strong and positive one—is essential to develop a healthy self-esteem. It is a valuable tool that affects our daily self-dialogue and reinforces our most intimate beliefs, attitudes, and feelings about ourselves.

Our mindset also determines our success or failure. According to a Stanford psychologist Carol Dweck, what we believe in majorly affects what we want and what we get. To Dweck, it is mindset that identifies our success and achievements. She suggests two types of mindsets— growth and fixed. People possessing a fixed mindset are of the idea that their qualities are unchangeable and innate. Those who possess a growth mindset believe that their abilities tend to develop and consolidate with different opportunities, experiences, struggles, and commitment. Growth and fixed mindsets are actually two different types of beliefs that lead to different behaviors and their results.

A growth mindset enables a person to recognize their abilities and to have a belief that they can learn and grow and is the basic key to success. The growth mindset could help children in schools when given assignments and tasks to perform. It lets them take things as a challenge and an opportunity to learn and grow positively. As a result, children could contribute to high achievements out of top efforts.

However, with adults, a growth mindset performs more or less the same but in a different manner. For example, one could face difficulties in finding a job. But a growth mindset could help them show high resilience and determination for achieving their goal. Such people are more likely to perform better in hard times. They have a constant hunger for learning and a wish to keep on exploring new things. Even if they fail or lose, they don't give up easily; in fact, they take it as an opportunity to grow more and bring out in them a better change.

People with a fixed mindset tend to give up easily because, in certain stressful situations, they think that it is the end of the world. Dweck explained that people of a fixed mindset are often waiting for an approval or a go-ahead to proceed. They feel that their personality is being judged based on their actions and behavior. To them, every situation calls for a confirmation of their existence.

Beliefs and Mindsets

Mindsets aren't merely beliefs. In fact, these beliefs are what determine our actions and ability. In the words of Tony Robbins, "A belief is simply a feeling of certainty about something." For instance, if you feel that you are intelligent, you become confident about it. Basically, it is the ideas that give birth to a belief. When you keep on adding your experiences to the ideas in your mind, a belief is formed. Thus, it is essential for us to know the roots or the core idea behind a belief.

Attitude and Mindset

Author Kendra Cherry stated in one of her books,

Psychologists define attitudes as a learned tendency to evaluate things in a certain way. This can include evaluations of people, issues, objects, or events. Such evaluations are often positive or negative, but they can also be uncertain at times. For example, you might have mixed feelings about a particular person or issue.

Cherry suggests that attitude consists in three basic elements (i.e., the emotional element, the cognitive element, and the behavioral element). The emotional element of an attitude determines how a person, object, or event makes you feel. The cognitive element caters to the thoughts and beliefs about a situation or a person, while the behavioral element includes how your attitude affects your behavior.

It is your mindset that shapes your attitude, which is how you feel about different things in your life while your attitude strengthens your mindset. At the same time, your beliefs create your attitude, which begets your mindset.

According to Mindset.com, "Mindsets are those collection of beliefs and thoughts that make up the mental attitude, inclination, habit or disposition that predetermines a person's interpretations and responses to events, circumstances, and situations."

Why Does Mindset Matter?

We can observe two types of people around us, those who seem to shine in almost every walk of life and those who cannot merely get things done no matter how much effort they exert. Studies suggest that it all depends on the way they think and act. Whatever a person believes they can achieve, and things start to happen for them in that particular retrospect. Those who doubt their abilities and circumstances face failures.

Failure is not a bad thing to experience. Loss and failure could be another form of opportunity for one to rise again better than before, tending not to make the same mistakes again. However, it is all a matter of having a certain mindset.

Mindset for Success

There is a psychological trait that all successful people appear to have in common. It has been cosigned by Bill Gates, while NASA uses it as a criterion for selecting potential systems engineers. This is the concept of the growth mindset, which is the better one for becoming successful.

As discussed earlier, the growth mindset is the belief that intelligence and skills in any field can be developed. But it is no magic. It will not help you get everything that you want out of life, and it won't make you the next Steve Jobs or Elon Musk. However, it is a powerful lens with which you can see the world and improve the probability of your success.

Almost all of us possess a blend of both growth and fixed mindsets. In some areas of our lives, we operate with a growth mindset, while in others we go with a fixed mindset. It is like a pair of glasses that are used at different times by a person. However, the growth mindset should be preferred most of the time.

Studies also suggest that people with a growth mindset are more successful than people with a fixed mindset. Growth mindset people are more resilient, which allows them to overcome challenges in life. They prioritize growing over failure and believe that they are always in a state of flux and transformation. So they don't attach their identity to their results.

Some people may deny that the growth mindset seems to map nicely onto reality. We know that the brain can continue to learn until the day we die, thanks to the field of neuroscience. It also seems quite intuitive that people must work hard and persevere, despite the obstacles, to end up being successful.

So the growth mindset seems to be a much more accurate view of reality than the fixed mindset. Growth mindset people are living in greater accordance with reality than fixed mindset people. They can make more accurate decisions, whereas fixed mindset people live in a greater state of delusion. What does it actually mean?

Imagine two entrepreneurs. One has a growth mindset, and the other has a fixed mindset. They are both in the initial phases of their entrepreneurial journey. Suddenly, they both encounter a roadblock and are forced to make a critical decision. The fixed mindset entrepreneur sees the long and arduous journey ahead due to the obstacle. The journey is in the way of what matters to them—the results. He believes that entrepreneurship should come easy to those who are destined for it. So he decides to quit.

The growth mindset entrepreneur also sees the long and arduous journey ahead and smiles. The journey is the way for him because it is what matters. So he accepts the long path and allows himself to mold into the person he wants to become to achieve the results he desires. So he decides to persist.

Looking at this example, most of us will agree that the entrepreneur with the growth mindset has a greater understanding of reality. His decision is more accurate. We know that things take time, effort, and a strategy to achieve, but it is often difficult to put that positive thinking into practice.

How to Develop a Growth Mindset?

The first key to developing a growth mindset is very simple. Believing that it exists and that it is possible for the brain to change is the first thing to do. Neuroscience has shown that our brains are not fixed; in fact, they are very malleable, so we can always grow and learn new skills.

A study found that a taxicab driver develops more gray matter in his brain to help him navigate more effectively in large cities. They also found that the amount of gray matter present in the brains of taxicab drivers was correlated with the number of years that they had been working as a taxi driver. This suggested that the act of driving a taxi led to changes in their brains, which allowed them to be more effective at their job.

The second key is to focus on the *process* over *results*. Dweck says that we should praise others highly for their efforts and processes rather than achievements. For example, it is better to say, "You worked on the presentation effectively to pitch the client that your hard work paid off well," rather than saying, "You are so smart that you got that client on board." In the preceding example, we focused on praising the person's effort or process of making a presentation for the client, which is controllable. Hopefully, they will learn to associate themselves and their results with that process. In the latter example, we praised the person for the result, which is out of their control. Unfortunately, this person will likely begin to associate themselves with the result.

It is, therefore, important to emphasize that it is not easy to pass a growth mindset on to others. It is not as simple as telling someone that they are hard workers and just need to put in the effort. Instead, they need to internalize that they can change their results by improving their process. So they need to know how to effectively create a process, alter it, and produce some effective results from it.

For me, the solution to this is to keep a journal. As an entrepreneur, you can pick an activity that you want to excel in as an effort to put into your business. For example, a salon owner wants to get good at working on an Excel sheet. He should write down a process in the journal that includes the steps for learning. After taking down the steps, he should put a quantifiable measurement to as many things as he can. In other words, his process is solidified when everything is quantified.

Next, he would need a result or a target to aim at. Let's say that he wants to work correctly on Excel for at least 60 percent in three weeks. This is the objective. So after three weeks, he can measure his progress with the set objective.

This method of keeping a journal, creating a process, and refining it until the desired outcome is achieved will help promote a growth mindset. It will keep the mind focused on a changeable process, while the results are measured and paid attention to only as an indicator of how well our process works. The process either works as intended or doesn't, but it says nothing of the person. The process is always malleable.

Another excellent idea is to seek advice from peers or seniors. You can look for the people having experience in the same field as they know how to tackle situations that you are already going through. You can get advice from them and see how yours measures up. You might find things that they do, or have done, interesting and easy to adopt. You can also read books about people you admire and try to find details about their process that you can incorporate into your own.

Last, accept challenges. To have a chance of fostering the growth mindset, you have to step outside of your comfort zone. People who don't leave their comfort zone begin to believe that their success is due to innate talent because everything comes so easy to them. For example, an IT company owner who has never been challenged in the market will begin to believe that he is a natural. As his business keeps on flourishing, it will make him ignore the process of putting in efforts. Unfortunately, all he sees is the result, so he gets attached to it. When he inevitably undergoes a loss, he will think that he isn't clever enough to take control. He will lose faith in himself because he isn't getting the desired results anymore.

On the other hand, going outside of your comfort zone forces you to adopt the growth mindset to avoid shattering under the weight of adversity. You have to focus on and adjust the process because you may not achieve the result you desire with your current process.

As an entrepreneur, you need to keep in mind that it takes a lot of effort to develop and that it will always be a battle to avoid falling into the fixed mindset. People will say certain things, or certain things will happen, that trigger a fixed mindset in us. So notice when this is happening and try to avoid getting fixed in place. Carol Dweck said, "The path to a growth mindset is a lifelong journey, not a proclamation."

Become the author of your own life by changing your mindset. Embracing a growth mindset will be a step ahead in the right direction. You need to practice it until it becomes second nature. You will notice that the fear of falling into the fixed mindset hole will automatically fade away. As an entrepreneur, you need to lead by example and show everyone around you how far you can go to achieve your goals, adopting the growth mindset in your life.

Entrepreneurial Mindset

An entrepreneurial mindset is about possessing the skill set that empowers people to recognize and avail of the opportunities, find effective solutions to the problems, learn from mistakes, and respond successfully to any sort of situation. To start a business, an entrepreneurial mindset is one of the best. People with an entrepreneurial mindset possess certain traits that include the following:

- Decisiveness
- Confidence
- Positive mental attitude
- Accountability
- Creativity and innovation
- Persuasive communication
- Active listening
- Determination and focus
- Resilience
- Self-drive
- Humility

Tips to Develop an Entrepreneurial Mindset

It doesn't matter if you are not born with an entrepreneurial mindset because you can develop it with time-tested tips given below:

Setting Clear Goals

It all starts with a plan wherein you set goals. Setting goals is essential because it is the mark that will help you find and decide your strategies to hit that mark. There should be no rush, so take enough time to set your goals.

Informed Decision

Becoming an entrepreneur is not guesswork but a conscious effort. Thus, conduct research and due diligence and weigh the pros and cons of your decision before finalizing it.

Learn from Your Failures

Failing is just a part of your effort to succeed eventually. Failures tell you what you must not do to get what you want to achieve. Thus, take your failures as learning tools and find a better strategy to move forward.

Be Committed

On top of all is your level of commitment. Of course, there will be many challenges on your way to becoming a health-care entrepreneur, and it is your commitment that will decide your journey and future. So be strongly committed to your vision and keep going on. Your commitment will help you see the issues from various angles and find practical solutions.

As you follow these steps, you will soon develop a strong entrepreneurial mindset.

REFERENCES

1. https://www.medicalnewstoday.com/articles/317321.
2. https://www.senate.gov/artandhistory/history/common/generic/FreedmensBureau.htm.
3. https://www.history.com/topics/great-depression/new-deal.
4. https://www.pbs.org/newshour/health/november-19-1945-harry-truman-calls-national-health-insurance-program.
5. https://www.chicagomag.com/city-life/october-2012/how-the-ama-scared-us-away-from-socialized-medicine-and-prepared-us-for-obamacare/.
6. https://www.thelancet.com/journals/lancet/article/PIIS0140-6736(15)61400-3/fulltext.
7. https://khn.org/news/kennedy-health-care-timeline/.
8. https://pubmed.ncbi.nlm.nih.gov/7989016/.
9. https://www.nytimes.com/2010/03/24/health/policy/24health.html.
10. https://en.wikipedia.org/wiki/American Association for Labor Legislation.
11. https://www.healthcare-now.org/legislation/wagner-murray-dingell-bill-of-1943/.
12. https://nerdfighteria.info/v/yN-MkRcOJjY/.
13. https://www.cnbc.com/2019/02/11/this-is-the-real-reason-most-americans-file-for-bankruptcy.html.
14. https://www.nytimes.com/2009/03/05/us/politics/05obama-text.html.
15. https://www.healthaffairs.org/doi/full/10.1377/hlthaff.2017.1299.
16. https://www.ehealthinsurance.com/resources/small-business/how-many-americans-get-health-insurance-from-their-employer.

17. https://www.cnbc.com/2018/01/18/few-americans-have-enough-savings-to-cover-a-1000-emergency.html.
18. https://www.washingtonpost.com/news/to-your-health/wp/2014/06/16/once-again-u-s-has-most-expensive-least-effective-health-care-system-in-survey/.
19. https://www.mckinsey.com/business-functions/operations/our-insights/decoding-digital-transformation-in-construction.
20. https://www.aacc.org/cln/cln-stat/2015/january/22/survey-assesses-global-healthcare-concerns.
21. https://samples.jblearning.com/0763763802/63800_CH01_Final.pdf.
22. https://www.businessinsider.com/theranos-and-other-healthcare-startups-that-failed-and-why-2019-3.
23. https://www.bloomberg.com/news/articles/2021-03-04/martin-shkreli-accused-of-drug-monopoly-scheme-by-insurer.
24. https://www.investopedia.com/articles/investing/020116/theranos-fallen-unicorn.asp.
25. https://www.worldometers.info/coronavirus/coronavirus-death-toll/.
26. https://www.cbinsights.com/research/tech-giants-digital-healthcare-investments/.
27. https://www.hipaajournal.com/april-2021-healthcare-data-breach-report/.
28. https://www.zolgensma.com/.
29. https://www.biospace.com/article/gene-therapy-zolgensma-tops-goodrx-list-of-10-most-expensive-drugs/.
30. https://en.wikipedia.org/wiki/Health_Insurance_Portability_and_Accountability_Act.
31. https://vsee.com/what-is-telemedicine/.
32. https://www.sdglobaltech.com/blog/10-brilliant-examples-of-wearables-in-healthcare.
33. https://www.sintec-project.eu/future-market-opportunities-for-wearable-devices/.
34. https://www.medicaleconomics.com/view/whats-ruining-medicine-physicians-paperwork-and-administrative-burdens.
35. https://blog.definitivehc.com/5-reasons-why-healthcare-costs-are-rising.
36. https://www.ama-assn.org/about/research/trends-health-care-spending.
37. https://www.healthcarefinancenews.com/news/cms-predicts-health-care-spending-will-skyrocket-6-trillion-2027.

38. https://blog.definitivehc.com/5-reasons-why-healthcare-costs-are-rising.
39. https://catalyst.nejm.org/doi/full/10.1056/CAT.17.0558.
40. https://info.intelichart.com/blog/barriers-to-value-based-care-and-how-to-overcome-them.
41. https://www.selecthub.com/medical-software/ehr-implementation-cost/.
42. https://courses.minia.edu.eg//Attach/10965Admin%20Post%20System%20(6).pdf.
43. https://ciolook.com/10-business-ideas-that-can-make-you-an-entrepreneur-in-2021/.
44. https://www.nerdwallet.com/article/small-business/health-care-business-ideas.
45. https://www.gdrc.org/icm/micro/what-is.html.
46. https://data.oecd.org/entrepreneur/enterprises-by-business-size.htm.
47. https://smallbusiness.chron.com/schedule-c-sole-proprietorship-60179.html.
48. https://businesstown.com/articles/the-pros-and-cons-of-a-sole-proprietorship/.
49. https://www.investopedia.com/terms/l/llc.asp.
50. https://www.allbusiness.com/pros-and-cons-of-a-limited-liability-company-llc-2517-1.html.
51. https://byjus.com/commerce/what-is-partnership/.
52. https://corporatedirect.com/start-a-business/entity-types/s-corporation/.
53. https://www.inc.com/guides/starting-a-c-corp.html.
54. https://www.fundera.com/blog/professional-corporation.
55. https://www.nwcphp.org/docs/feasibility/feasibility_plan_print.pdf.
56. https://www.mindtools.com/pages/article/newTMC_05.htm.
57. https://sustainablemarketing.com.au/public-relations/public-relations-plan.
58. https://www.investopedia.com/terms/l/loyalty-program.asp.
59. https://courses.lumenlearning.com/wmopen-introductiontobusiness/chapter/management-theory/.
60. https://revcycleintelligence.com/news/exploring-the-role-of-supply-chain-management-in-healthcare.
61. https://www.ncbi.nlm.nih.gov/pmc/articles/PMC7732404/.
62. https://www.medicaldevice-network.com/features/top-medical-device-companies/.

63. https://news.lenovo.com/the-human-centric-rise-of-artificial-intelligence-in-healthcare/.
64. https://digitalsurgery.com/.
65. https://owkin.com/platform/loop/.
66. https://medicalchain.com/en/.
67. https://www.iryo.io/.
68. https://codete.com/blog/chatbots-in-healthcare.
69. https://blog.bitext.com/nlu-vs.-itr-chatbots...-which-one-should-i-use
70. https://visualise.com/virtual-reality/virtual-reality-healthcare.
71. https://www.ohsu.edu/school-of-medicine/medical-informatics-and-clinical-epidemiology/data-science-and-dmice.
72. https://www.ncbi.nlm.nih.gov/pmc/articles/PMC2814957/.
73. https://www.amia.org/about-amia/science-informatics.
74. https://www.brown.edu/academics/medical/about-us/research/centers-institutes-and-programs/biomedical-informatics/.
75. https://about.kaiserpermanente.org/our-story/our-history/kp-northern-california-marks-half-a-century-of-stellar-research.
76. https://www.sas.com/en_us/insights/analytics/data-mining.html.
77. https://www.zentut.com/data-mining/data-mining-techniques/.
78. https://www.healthcatalyst.com/enable-knowledge-management-in-healthcare.
79. https://www.researchgate.net/publication/283621788_Total_Quality_Management_in_Healthcare.
80. https://www.ahrq.gov/ncepcr/tools/pf-handbook/mod4.html.

Professor Chris Ehiobuche writes books and peer-review journal articles on management, business, global business, education, health care, and sustainability for youths, adults, and professionals. With over fifty high-level journal publications and five books, he is twice a Best Author awardee of Franklin Publishers. His research currently focuses on health-care entrepreneurship, innovations and technology's impact on health-care delivery, paradigm changes, and the future of small independent primary care practitioners. His recent scholarship includes:

- "The Impact of COVID-19 Pandemic on the Management of Private Medical Office Practices: A Conundrum," Western Journal of Human Resource Management 19, no. 1 (Fall 2020)
- "A Critical Perspective on Industry Involvement in Higher Education Learning: Enhancing Graduates' Knowledge and Skills for Job Creation in Nigeria Industry and Higher Education." First published online on April 29, 2020
- "Women Entrepreneurship and Poverty Alleviation in Nigeria," Journal of Small Business and Entrepreneurship Development, RSBE2020-0163.

When he is not teaching or writing, he does management consulting and business development in and outside the USA. He likes soccer and cooking. Professor Ehiobuche is the current chair of the Master of Business Administration in Health-Care Administration and Leadership program at Stockton University, Atlantic City, New Jersey.

Made in the USA
Middletown, DE
02 September 2024

60134907R00106